Lecture Notes of the Institute
for Computer Sciences, Social Informatics
and Telecommunications Engineering   270

More information about this series at http://www.springer.com/series/8197

Honghao Gao · Yuyu Yin
Xiaoxian Yang · Huaikou Miao (Eds.)

Testbeds and Research Infrastructures for the Development of Networks and Communities

13th EAI International Conference, TridentCom 2018
Shanghai, China, December 1–3, 2018
Proceedings

Editors
Honghao Gao
Shanghai University
Shanghai, China

Xiaoxian Yang
Shanghai Second Polytechnic University
Shanghai, China

Yuyu Yin
Hangzhou Dianzi University
Hangzhou, Zhejiang, China

Huaikou Miao
Shanghai University
Shanghai, China

ISSN 1867-8211 ISSN 1867-822X (electronic)
Lecture Notes of the Institute for Computer Sciences, Social Informatics
and Telecommunications Engineering
ISBN 978-3-030-12970-5 ISBN 978-3-030-12971-2 (eBook)
https://doi.org/10.1007/978-3-030-12971-2

Library of Congress Control Number: 2019931004

This Springer imprint is published by the registered company Springer Nature Switzerland AG
The registered company address is: Gewerbestrasse 11, 6330 Cham, Switzerland

Preface

We are delighted to introduce the proceedings of the 13th European Alliance for Innovation (EAI) International Conference on Testbeds and Research Infrastructures for the Development of Networks and Communities (TridentCom 2018). This conference brought together technical experts and researchers from academic and industry from all around the world to discuss the emerging technologies of big data, cyber-physical systems, and computer communications.

The technical program of TridentCom 2018 consisted of ten full papers. The conference sessions were: Session 1, Wireless and Testbed Application; Session 2, Uncertainty Analytics and Formal Verification; and Session 3, Knowledge Graph. Aside from the high-quality technical paper presentations, the technical program also featured two keynote speeches given by Dr. Zhi Wang from Zhejiang University and Dr. Yang Yang from Shanghai Tech University.

Coordination with the steering chair, Imrich Chlamtac, was essential for the success of the conference. We sincerely appreciate his constant support and guidance. It was also a great pleasure to work with such an excellent Organizing Committee team for their hard work in organizing and supporting the conference. In particular, we thank the Technical Program Committee, led by our TPC co-chairs, Dr. Yuyu Yin and Dr. Xiaoxian Yang, who completed the peer-review process of technical papers and created a high-quality technical program. We are also grateful to the conference manager, Andrea Piekova, for her support and to all the authors who submitted their papers to the TridentCom 2018 conference.

We strongly believe that TridentCom provides a good forum for researchers, developers, and practitioners to discuss all science and technology aspects that are relevant to big data, cyber-physical systems, and computer communications. We also expect that future TridentCom conferences will be as successful and stimulating, as indicated by the contributions presented in this volume.

January 2019

Honghao Gao
Huaikou Miao

The original version of the book was revised: The title of the book has been corrected. The correction to the book is available at https://doi.org/10.1007/978-3-030-12971-2_11

Organization

Steering Committee

Imrich Chlamtac   Bruno Kessler Professor, University of Trento, Italy

Organizing Committee

General Co-chairs

Honghao Gao   Shanghai University, China
Huaikou Miao   Shanghai University, China

Technical Program Committee Co-chairs

Yuyu Yin   Hangzhou Dianzi University, China
Xiaoxian Yang   Shanghai Polytechnic University, China

Web Chair

Wanqiu Huang   Shanghai University, China

Publicity and Social Media Chair

Yuan Tao   Shanghai University, China

Workshops Chair

Yucong Duan   Hainan University, China

Publications Chair

Youhuizi Li   Hangzhou Dianzi University, China

Local Chair

Qiming Zuo   Shanghai University, China

Conference Manager

Andrea Piekova   EAI, Italy

Technical Program Committee

Abdelrahman Osman Elfaki   University of Tabuk, Saudi Arabia
Ajay Kattepur   Tata Consultancy Services
Alex Norta   Tallinn University of Technology, Estonia

Amit Dvir	Budapest University of Technology and Economics, Hungary
Antonella Longo	University of Salento, Italy
Chengzhong Xu	Wayne State University, USA
Guoray Cai	Pennsylvania State University, USA
Honghao Gao	Shanghai University, China
Hong-Linh Truong	Vienna University of Technology, Austria
Huaikou Miao	Shanghai University, China
HuiYuan Zheng	Macquarie University
Jiangchuan Liu	Simon Fraser University, Canada
Jiannong Cao	Hong Kong Polytechnic University, SAR China
Jianwei Yin	Zhejiang University, China
Jianwen Su	University of California, USA
Jian Zhao	Institute for Infocomm Research, Singapore
Jia Zhang	Northern Illinois University, USA
Jilin Zhang	Hangzhou Dianzi University, China
Jingyu Zhang	University of Sydney, Australia
Joe Tekli	Lebanese American University, Lebanon
Jue Wang	Supercomputing Center of the China Academy of Sciences, China
Klaus-Dieter Schewe	Information Science Research Centre
Kumiko Tadano	Nippon Electric Company
Lai Xu	Bournemouth University, UK
Lei Liu	Karlsruhe Institute of Technology, Germany
Li Kuang	Hangzhou Normal University, China
Limin Shen	Yanshan University, China
Marco Comerio	University of Milano-Bicocca, Italy
Nanjangud C. Narendra	MS Ramaiah University of Applied Sciences, India
Nianjun Joe Zhou	IBM Thomas J. Watson Research Center, USA
Peng Di	The University of New South Wales, Australia
Qiang Duan	Pennsylvania State University, USA
Qing Wu	Hangzhou Dianzi University, China
Robert Lagerstrom	KTH Royal Institute of Technology, Sweden
Shuiguang Deng	ZheJiang University, China
Stephan Reiff-Marganiec	University of Leicester, UK
Stephen Wang	Toshiba Telecommunications Research Laboratory Europe
Wan Tang	South-Central University for Nationalities
Xiaofei Zhang	Hong Kong University of Science and Technology, SAR China
Yi Wang	Macquarie University, Australia
Yucong Duan	Hainan University, China
YuYu Yin	Hangzhou Dianzi University, China
Zhou Su	Waseda University, Japan

Contents

Knowledge Graph

Wireless and Testbed Application

Indriya2: A Heterogeneous Wireless Sensor Network (WSN) Testbed

Paramasiven Appavoo$^{(\boxtimes)}$, Ebram Kamal William, Mun Choon Chan,
and Mobashir Mohammad

National University of Singapore, Singapore, Singapore
{pappavoo,ebramkw,chanmc,mobashir}@comp.nus.edu.sg

Abstract. Wireless sensor network testbeds are important elements of
sensor network/IoT research. The Indriya testbed has been serving the
sensor network community for the last 8 years. Researchers from more
than a hundred institutions around the world have been actively using
the testbed in their work. However, given that Indriya has been deployed
for over 8 years, it has a number of limitations. For example, it lacks support for heterogeneous devices and the ability to handle data generated
by the testbed with no loss, even at a relatively low sampling rate. In
this paper, we present the design and implementation of an upgraded
version of Indriya, Indriya2, with the following improvements, namely
(1) support for heterogeneous sensor devices, (2) support for higher data
rate through the infrastructure, (3) support for multiple users to schedule jobs over non-overlapping set of heterogeneous nodes at the same
time, and (4) a real-time publish/subscribe architecture to send/receive
data to/from the testbed nodes.

Keywords: Testbed · Internet of Things · Wireless sensor network

1 Introduction

With the emergence of Internet-of-Things (IoT), the ability to experiment and
evaluate different sensor network protocols in large, realistic environments con-
tinued to be important. Indriya [1], is a wireless sensor network testbed deployed
at the School of Computing, National University of Singapore. Indriya has been
available as an open testbed for use by the research communities for more than
8 years (since December 2009). It has served more than 500 users from over 150
institutions with over 13,000 jobs executed.

While Indriya has served its purpose well, it has limitations. First, its software
is derived from MoteLab [18], an even older wireless sensor network testbed and
much of the internal design is based on software tools and components that are
very dated. This makes system upgrade and maintenance difficult. Second, the
current design of Indriya can support only one single hardware platform (TelsoB
[4]). With many new sensor hardware platforms available in the last few years

© ICST Institute for Computer Sciences, Social Informatics and Telecommunications Engineering 2019
Published by Springer Nature Switzerland AG 2019. All Rights Reserved
H. Gao et al. (Eds.): TridentCom 2018, LNICST 270, pp. 3–19, 2019.
https://doi.org/10.1007/978-3-030-12971-2_1

and with more likely to emerge in the future, it is important that the testbed is able to support newer hardware platforms.

In this paper, we present the design of Indriya2. Indriya2 is designed to address the limitations of Indriya and has the following objectives. First, it should be able to support different sensor platforms and wireless network technologies. Second, the infrastructure should support higher data rate to handle high influx of time-stamped data generated by nodes for either debugging or application purposes. The need to support higher aggregated data rate comes from the possible increase in either number of sensor nodes in the testbed or higher traffic rate generated to support experimentation.

We have completed the design and implementation of Indriya2. The main features are summarized as follow:

1. It can support different hardware platforms. Currently, Indriya2 can support a mixture of TelosB, SensorTag CC2650 and SensorTag CC1350. New device types can be easily added to the testbed by adding a small device specific components for flashing. Indriya2 also supports different operating systems (TinyOS [19] and Contiki [20]) and wireless network technologies (BLE and IEEE 802.15.4g).
2. The internal design of Indriya2 has been completely overhauled to improve software portability and overall performance. It uses a time-series database, InfluxDB, that supports high influx of streaming sensor data. Experiments show that the database can easily support over 2000 transactions per second running on a mid-range commodity server.
3. The front-end interface allows multiple users to run multiple experiments at the same time using different set of nodes. For real-time sensor data monitoring, all the data generated by the active nodes, i.e. under running experiments, are available in real-time through a MQTT server.

The paper is organized as follows. We briefly presented related work in Sect. 2 and recap the design of Indriya in Sect. 3. The design and user interface of Indriya2 are covered in Sect. 4 and 5 respectively. Testbed results are presented in Sect. 6 and conclusion in Sect. 7.

2   Related Work

In this section, we will give a short description of the other common testbeds for wireless sensor networking that are popular in the research community.

FlockLab [14] is a wireless sensor network testbed developed and run by the Computer Engineering and Networks Laboratory at the Swiss Federal Institute of Technology Zurich in Switzerland with TinyNode184, Tmote Sky (TelosB), Opal, OpenMote, and MSP430-CCRF as the sensor motes. It provides reliable power and energy measurements while JamLab [15] allows for generation and reproduction of interference patterns.

FIT IoT-LAB [16] is a large scale infrastructure for wireless sensor networks developed by a consortium of five French institutions of higher education and research with over 2000 nodes using WSN430, M3, and A8 as the sensor platform. One unique feature of the IoT-LAB is that it includes mobile robots.

The TKN WIreless NetworkS Testbed (TWIST) [17] is developed by the Telecommunication Networks Group (TKN) at the Technische Universität Berlin. TWIST uses 46 single-board and wall-powered computers to manage 204 testbed nodes. Sensor nodes include both the TmoteSky and eyesIFXv2 nodes.

Indriya2 mostly uses the same USB wiring and hardware infrastructure as Indriya. The major changes are in the software design and architecture which allows more support for requirements of an Internet of Things platform, including heterogeneous hardware that supports different wireless technology, and timestamped data access through MQTT service.

3 Indriya

Indriya is deployed across three different floors of our main School of Computing building (COM1). Indriya2's deployment remains the same. The deployment covers spaces used for different purposes, including laboratories, tutorial rooms, seminar rooms, study areas, and walkways. The backend is based on a cluster-based design with each cluster consisting of a single cluster-head. The motes are connected to the cluster-head using USB hubs and active USB cables. The cluster-heads are connected to a server via Ethernet. The server manages the testbed and provides a user interface.

Over the past 8 years, Indriya has registered more than 500 users from more than 150 institutions and over 25 countries. More than 65% of the users are from overseas, including India, Germany, Switzerland, Sweden, United Kingdom and Brazil. The total number of jobs scheduled exceeds 13,000 averaging more than 1,400 per year.

Due to the deployment inside a very active university building, the devices experience real world interference from coexisting WiFi operating in the 2.4 GHz spectrum. This give the users a very realistic testbed to try out and improve their protocols. Besides interference, due to the 3 dimensional deployment of nodes across the three levels of the building, the communication suffers from random occlusion from different objects, giving constantly changing topologies of up to 7 hops at maximum transmission power.

In spite of its popular usage, there are a number of limitations to Indriya's design and implementation. We highlight some of the issues below.

- The design is tightly coupled with TinyOS [2] infrastructure, whose latest release is dated August 2012. Additional class files are required to properly format the output.
- The MySQL database used is not suited for high influx of time series data produced by the sensor network due to the combination of large number of sensor motes sending data on the back channel at (relatively) high rate.

- The system supports only one type of node, that is the CrossBow TelosB [4]. TelosB is a very old platform with limited sensors. The sensor data collected is also relatively noisy when compared to newer sensor hardware like the CC2650 SensorTag [3].
- The source is written in multiple programming languages including C, Perl, and PHP with numerous dependencies, making it difficult to maintain and update.

Indriya2 is designed to address these issues. We will present its design in the next two sections.

4   System Architecture

The system architecture for Indriya2 is shown in Fig. 1. The main components are (1) nodes, like TelosB, SensorTags cc2650, and others, (2) gateways, which are mini desktops like mac-mini and tiny-lenovo, and (3) server(s). Currently, the gateways for Indriya2 are 6 mac-minis running Ubuntu 14 and the server is a quad-core machine with 16 GB RAM running Ubuntu 16.

4.1   Hardware

In this section, we will show how Indriya2 is deployed at the School of Computing of National University of Singapore. Figure 2 shows a picture of cc2650

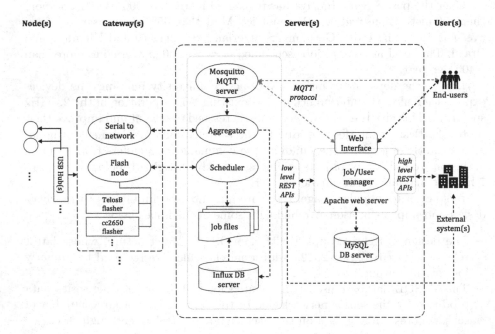

Fig. 1. System architecture of Indriya2

as deployed in the building. Figure 3 shows the gateway connected to the USB hubs and the active cables at the ceiling of the building.

4.2 Gateway Sub-components

The nodes are connected to the gateways via USB hubs. The gateways see the devices with unique names under linux directory system of "/dev/serial/by-id/". For each type of device, the appropriate flasher application program is used to flash a particular device, based on its physical ID, with the user program. The flasher [5] used for flashing the TelosB can also be used for the Zolertia Z1 [6] and Arago Systems WisMote [7]. As for the SensorTags, the standalone flasher generated from the standard Uniflash interface [8], provided by the manufacturer (Texas Instrument), is used. It can flash other types of nodes from the same family including CC13xx, CC25xx, CC26xx, CC3220, CC3120, and others. Adding a new device category requires only adding, if needed, a new flasher program.

The data generated by the user programs are transmitted through the serial port to the network port using the **ser2net** program. The current version used [9] allows for multiple connections, whenever required, unlike the default version provided in the Linux installation. All the devices are uniquely mapped to a network port based on their physical ID. Table 1 shows the permanent ID used for the device as opposed to connection/temporary ID, which varies, as it is assigned at connection time. The table also shows excerpts for two types of devices, namely TelosB and CC2650, and their respective settings and configurations.

Given that a network port is associated with the serial data port of the device, a remote server program, namely the **aggregator** in our architecture, can connect to any selected node, identified by its network port and gateway IP address.

4.3 Server Sub-components

The main sub-components of the server are as follows:

Aggregator. The aggregator retrieves data from the nodes generated by the active job(s). One copy of the data is forwarded to the database (Influx DB) another copy is published to the appropriate active users via the MQTT server. The latter allows end-users to view in real-time, the output of the nodes. End-users can also push data to the nodes via the MQTT server. The facility to pull and push data enable applications that have both monitor and control requirements, include those that perform feedback control.

Scheduler. The scheduler starts/ends the jobs at the scheduled times. If the job is successfully started, the nodes' status change to active and the aggregator starts forwarding the data to the data store. In case a node encounters a flashing failure, retries are performed up to three times. At the end of a job, the nodes'

Fig. 2. Motes as deployed in the building.

status is changed to inactive and the data stored for that job into the Influx DB is zipped and archived on the file system.

The Python Event Scheduler [10] was used, running on time resolution of microseconds.

Fig. 3. Gateway connected to USB hubs and active cables.

Table 1. Mapping device serial to TCP network port

Device type	Connection ID by device serial port in /dev/tty*	Permanent ID in /dev/serial/by-id	Map to TCP port	ser2net mapping configuration line
TelosB	/dev/ttyUSB0	/dev/serial/by-id /usb-XBOW_Crossbow _Telos_Rev.B_XBTNPM 52-if00-port0	4000	4000:raw:0:/dev/ serial/by-id/usb -XBOW_Crossbow_Telos_ Rev.B_XBTNPM52-if00- port0:115200, 8DATABITS,NONE, 1STOPBIT
CC2650	/dev/ttyACM0	/dev/serial/by-id/ usb-Texas_ Instruments_XDS110 _02.03.00.08_ Embed_with_CMSIS -DAP_L3002833-if00	4100	4100:raw:0:/dev/ serial/by-id/usb- Texas_Instruments_ XDS110_02.03.00.08 _Embed_with_CMSIS- DAP_L3002833-if00: 115200,8DATABITS, NONE,1STOPBIT
	/dev/ttyACM1	/dev/serial/by -id/usb-Texas_ Instruments_XDS110 _02.03.00.08_ Embed_with_CMSIS- DAP_L3002833-if03		

MQTT Server. The Mosquitto MQTT server [11] is used. The MQTT server allows the user or a remote program to process the data generated from the user's job in real-time. The user can also publish, i.e. send data, to a particular node which is part of his running job. While the MQTT ensures that legitimate users are allowed to publish, the aggregator makes sure that users only publish to node of their currently active jobs. The different levels of QoS supported by the server are **0** for at most once, **1** for at least once, and **2** for exactly once.

High Influx Database. Influx DB [12] is selected because of its ability to handle timestamped data at very high rate. Our evaluation shows that Influx DB meets our current and future requirements based on nodes capabilities to generate data at high rate. Note that sending records of timestamped data in batches, using JSON format over REST, allows for even higher data rate compare to writing records individually.

Job/User Manager. All users and respective job information are maintained using the MySQL DB. Upon user activation by the administrator, the former is given a limited quota of 30 min for scheduling jobs. Statistics on jobs scheduled can be viewed as well as editing jobs information and statistics is allowed.

REST APIs. The higher and lower levels of Indriya2 are loosely-coupled as shown in Fig. 1. The low level REST APIs allows for any form of interface as long as REST calls can be performed. Moreover, even the front-end can be accessed with REST APIs. This allows for smooth federation with other testbed platforms in the future if needed. To enhance security while using the REST APIs, using the API requires adding a timestamp token to the job schedule request to protect against replay attack. Hash value of the request is calculated and appended which is used to preserve the integrity. The request is encrypted using the user's MQTT credentials which preserve authenticity and confidentiality.

5   Executing a Job

In this section, we will describe the steps to create, schedule, and get the results from the job from the graphical user interface[1] as well as on the backend. After the user signs in, the user can create a job as shown in Fig. 4 where the user specifies the job name, chooses the mote-type, and selects the binary files to be used. In the next step, in Fig. 5, the user associates different binary files to different motes and creates the job. After creating the job, the user can schedule the job in a free time slot as shown in Fig. 6.

When it is time to execute a particular job, the scheduler locks the job so that its cancellation cannot be executed on that particular job during that time it is going to be flashed. This is done because once the flashing procedure is launched on the device, it cannot be interrupted. For each node to be flashed, a thread is launched that firstly uses **rsync**, without overwriting, to copy the

---

[1] https://indriya.comp.nus.edu.sg/.

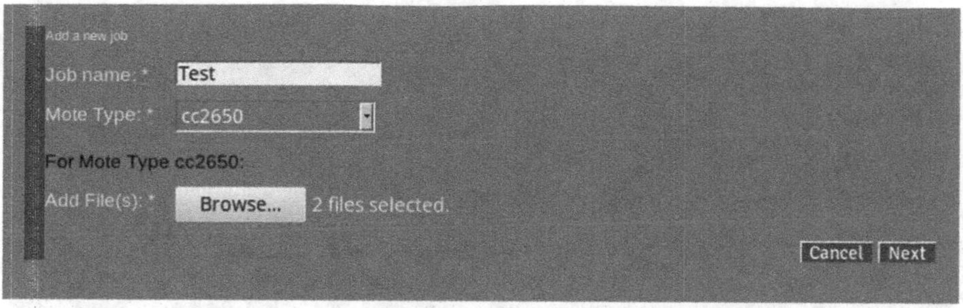

Fig. 4. Start creating a job.

required binary file to the respective gateway. Secondly, **ssh** is used to launch the appropriate flasher command with the required parameters to burn the binary files to the targeted nodes. The process is depicted in Fig. 7.

When an active user sends data to a node of his running job via the MQTT server, the latter checks whether the user is legitimate and the aggregator checks whether the running node is under that particular active user. The data is then pushed to the node by the aggregator through the network connection.

Finally, at the end of the job, the scheduler executes functions to: (1) set the status of the active users/nodes lists, so that the aggregator stops forwarding activities for the users/nodes related to that job, (2) retrieve the job's data from the Influx DB, zip and save it on the file system so that it can retrieved by the web server, and (3) run a maintenance job that flashes a default program to reset the node to a default behavior.

6   Evaluation

The wiring infrastructure of Indriya2 allows the installation of more than 140 sensor nodes. In this evaluation, the configuration has 102 motes out of which 74 are TelosBs and 28 are CC2650 sensortags. TelosB comes with an 8 MHz TI MSP430 microcontroller with 10 KB RAM and most of them have light, temperature and humidity sensors integrated. The CC2650 sensortag has an ARM Cortex-M3, reaching up to 48 MHz, with 28 KB SRAM. It has more sensors, including barometer, microphone, gyroscope, accelerometer, magnetometer by default.

In this section, we present two sets of experimental results. In the first set of experiments (Sect. 6.1 to 6.3) we present results on the network connectivity across the entire network as well as within each device cluster. In Sect. 6.4, we look at the performance of the MQTT server.

In order to measure network connectivity, we program each node to broadcast one packet every second for a total of 100 s each in a round robin fashion. When a node is not transmitting, it listens to the channel and records the packets, including the source of the packet and the received signal strength (RSS) of each packet. All packets are transmitted on channel 26. As each packet contains

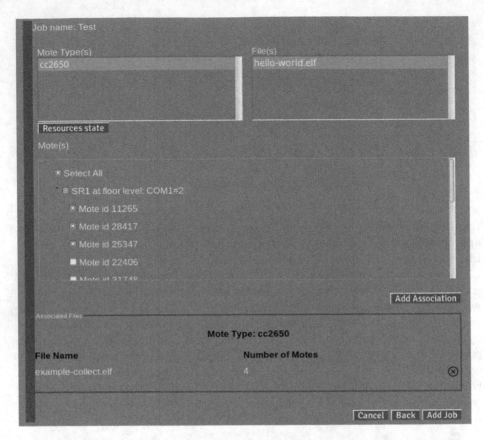

Fig. 5. Associate binary files to motes.

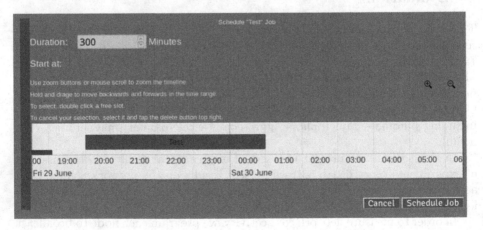

Fig. 6. Schedule a job.

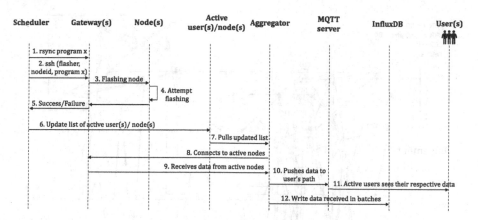

Fig. 7. Job execution process

a sequence number and we know the total number of packets transmitted by each node, we can compute the packet reception ratio (PRR) of the wireless link between two nodes.

6.1 Nodes' Connectivity

The network connectivity measured is shown in Fig. 8. Blue squares and red circles are used to denote CC2650s and TelosBs respectively. We used black solid links to indicate links with PRR greater than or equal to 0.8 and dotted lines for links with PRR between 0.5 and 0.8. Links with PRR less than 0.5 are not shown.

Tables 2 and 3 summarize the connectivity in different forms, considering links with different PRRs. We can make the following observations. First, connectivity is clearly not symmetric as in-degrees are different from out-degrees. Considering the case for PRR > 0.8, the median connectivity for TelosB and CC2650 are 6 and 4 respectively.

6.2 PRR and RSS Distribution

The overall link quality of the different clusters, based on PRR and RSS, are shown in Fig. 9. The skewness of the PRR distribution for both the CC2650 and TelosB clusters indicate that the link quality is either high or low. The RSS observed by the TelosB cluster is clearly centered at a lower dBm, while in general, the RSS observed is highest around −85 dBm.

6.3 Correlating Performance (PRR) with RSS

The correlation between RSS and PRR is useful for protocol that uses RSS to estimate the link quality (PRR). From Fig. 10, both the TelosB and the CC2650 clusters shows a clear correlation between higher PRR with higher RSS. However, it is also noted that there are some cases where the RSS is low but PRR is still high.

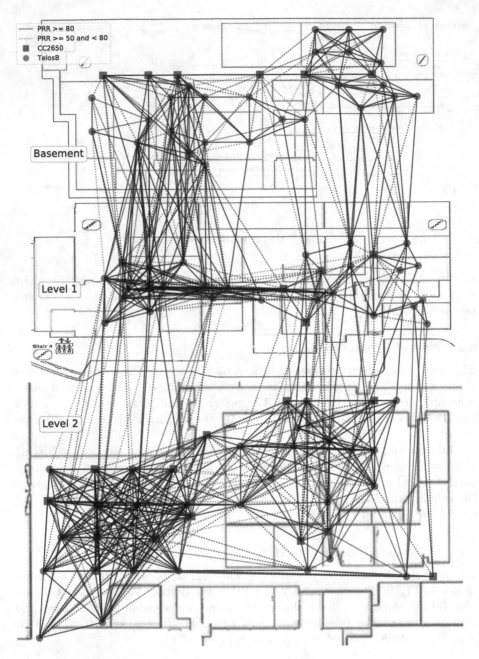

Fig. 8. Indriya2: Layout of the heterogeneous testbed.

Table 2. Nodes connectivity (PRR > 80)

Cluster		TelosB (74)	CC2650 (26)	Heterogeneous (102)
Link type	Percentile			
In-degree	10th percentile	3	1.5	4.1
	Median	6	4	9
	90th percentile	10	6	17
Out-degree	10th percentile	1.3	2	3.1
	Median	6	4	10
	90th percentile	11	7	17
Cluster density (0-1)		0.087	0.157	0.096

Table 3. Nodes connectivity (PRR > 50)

Cluster		TelosB (74)	CC2650 (28)	Heterogeneous (102)
Link type	Percentile			
In-degree	10th percentile	5	2	7
	Median	9	5	13
	90th percentile	13	8	20.9
Out-degree	10th percentile	3.3	2	5
	Median	9	5	13
	90th percentile	14	7	21.9
Cluster density (0-1)		0.123	0.187	0.136

6.4 Benchmarking for Scalability

Firstly, to evaluate the performance of the MQTT server, two tests were performed. In the first test, we want to find out how scalable is the testbed infrastructure as more nodes are added and each node may transmit at high data rate. Currently, a node on the testbed can generate on the average around 11,500 bytes (115 lines/samples of 100 bytes) on the serial port. The benchmarking tool from [13] was used. Evaluation shows that the system can support more than 500 nodes, each sending 115 messages of 100 bytes to our MQTT server.

In the second test, we compare the performance of MQTT subscription against a direct TCP connection with nodes generating data samples at approximately 120 Hz. This test compares the performance of using the publish/subscribe feature provided by MQTT to the approach of fetching data directly using TCP sockets. While the TCP connection carries only the data generated by the sensor (for the test we used <loadtest,nodeid,7041,1, this is a load test>), the content from our MQTT broker also adds some metadata, namely the timestamp and the node id of the source, as seen in the following

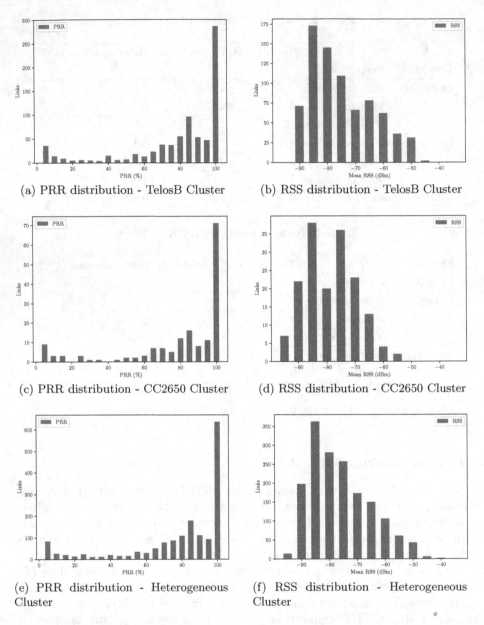

Fig. 9. PRR and RSS distribution for the TelosB cluster, CC2650 cluster and both combined as a heterogeneous cluster using the IEEE 802.15.4 standard.

< *"nodeid", "7041" "value": "loadtest,nodeid,7041,1, this is a load test", "time": "2018-06-29T12:35:45.731053Z"*>. In this experiment, the relative delay using the two modes of connection, to receive/subscribe to the data, are shown in Fig. 11.

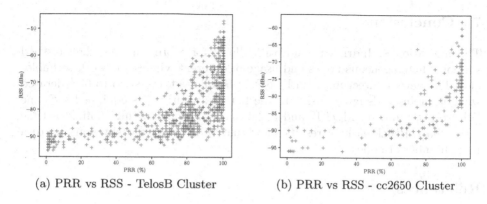

(a) PRR vs RSS - TelosB Cluster   (b) PRR vs RSS - cc2650 Cluster

Fig. 10. PRR vs RSS

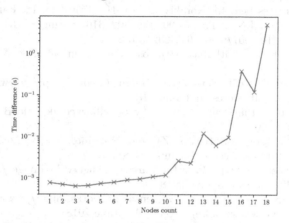

Fig. 11. Average delay between messages from MQTT subscription messages and direct TCP socket

In the evaluation, every two minutes, a node is added to the group of nodes that are generating data to the MQTT server and the average time difference taken over each sample received over the period preceding the arrival of the next node is computed and plotted. It is noted that after the arrival of the 16th and 17th nodes, the average time difference is still less than 500 ms. At that time, the total number of messages generated and received in one second is over 2000. This implies that the testbed can easily support 200 nodes generating data at 10 Hz, which is sufficient for most wireless sensor network applications.

For the evaluation of the Influx database, nearly 300 millions messages were generated and successfully recorded over a period of 4 h. This means that the system can support 200 nodes generating data at 100 Hz over a period of 4 h.

7   Conclusion

The migration of Indriya to Indriya2 allows for more features. The testbed supports heterogeneous nodes and usage of different wireless network technologies. The new architecture, with REST APIs, allows the system to be federated with other testbeds fairly easily. In the IoT era, Indriya2 is equipped with the lightweight protocol, MQTT, and a database allowing for high influx of time series data. Benchmarking results show that Indriya2 can easily scale up to a large number of nodes.

References

1. Doddavenkatappa, M., Chan, M.C., Ananda, A.L.: Indriya: a low-cost, 3D wireless sensor network testbed. In: Korakis, T., Li, H., Tran-Gia, P., Park, H.-S. (eds.) TridentCom 2011. LNICST, vol. 90, pp. 302–316. Springer, Heidelberg (2012). https://doi.org/10.1007/978-3-642-29273-6_23
2. TinyOS-main. https://github.com/tinyos/tinyos-main/releases. Accessed 4 June 2018
3. Multi-Standard CC2650 SensorTag Design Guide. http://www.ti.com/lit/ug/tidu862/tidu862.pdf. Accessed 4 June 2018
4. TelosB Mote Platform. https://www.willow.co.uk/TelosB_Datasheet.pdf. Accessed 4 June 2018
5. Python-msp430-tools for TelosB, Z1 and WisMote. https://github.com/cetic/python-msp430-tools. Accessed 5 June 2018
6. Z1 Datasheet. http://zolertia.sourceforge.net/wiki/images/e/e8/Z1_RevC_Datasheet.pdf. Accessed 5 June 2018
7. WiSNet: Complete solution for IPv6 sensor networks. http://www.aragosystems.com/produits/wisnet/wismote/. Accessed 5 June 2018
8. Uniflash Standalone Flash Tool for TI Microcontrollers (MCU), Sitara Processors & SimpleLink devices. http://www.ti.com/tool/UNIFLASH. Accessed 5 June 2018
9. Serial port to network proxy enhanced for multi-connections support! https://github.com/nickxia/ser2nets. Accessed 4 June 2018
10. Sched - Event scheduler. https://docs.python.org/3/library/sched.html. Accessed 4 June 2018
11. Eclipse Mosquitto^{TM}: An open source MQTT broker homepage. https://mosquitto.org/. Accessed 4 June 2018
12. InfluxDB homepage. https://docs.influxdata.com/influxdb. Accessed 4 June 2018
13. Simple MQTT (broker) benchmarking tool. https://github.com/krylovsk/mqtt-benchmark. Accessed 30 June 2018
14. Lim, R., Ferrari, F., Zimmerling, M., Walser, C., Sommer, P., Beutel, J.: FlockLab: a testbed for distributed, synchronized tracing and profiling of wireless embedded systems. In: Proceedings of the 12th International Conference on Information Processing in Sensor Networks, New York, pp. 153–166 (2013)
15. Boano, C.A., Voigt, T., Noda, C., Römer, K., Zúñiga, M.: JamLab: augmenting sensornet testbeds with realistic and controlled interference generation. In: Proceedings of the 10th ACM/IEEE International Conference on Information Processing in Sensor Networks, pp. 175–186 (2011)
16. Adjih, C., et al.: FIT IoT-LAB: a large scale open experimental IoT testbed. In: IEEE 2nd World Forum on Internet of Things (WFIoT), pp. 459–464 (2015)

17. Handziski, V., Köpke, A., Willig, A., Wolisz, A.: TWIST: a scalable and reconfigurable testbed for wireless indoor experiments with sensor networks. In: Proceedings of the 2nd International Workshop on Multi-hop Ad Hoc Networks: From Theory to Reality, pp. 63–70. ACM (2006)
18. Werner-Allen, G., Swieskowski, P., Welsh, M.: MoteLab: a wireless sensor network testbed. In: The Proceedings of the 4th International Symposium on Information Processing in Sensor Networks, p. 68 (2005)
19. Levis, P., et al.: TinyOS: an operating system for sensor networks. In: Weber, W., Rabaey, J.M., Aarts, E. (eds.) Ambient Intelligence. Springer, Heidelberg (2005). https://doi.org/10.1007/3-540-27139-2_7
20. Dunkels, A., Gronvall, B., Voigt, T.: Contiki-a lightweight and flexible operating system for tiny networked sensors. In: Local Computer Networks (2004)

Throughput Analytics of Data Transfer Infrastructures

Nageswara S. V. Rao[1(✉)], Qiang Liu[1], Zhengchun Liu[2],
Rajkumar Kettimuthu[2], and Ian Foster[2]

[1] Oak Ridge National Laboratory, Oak Ridge, TN, USA
{raons,liuq1}@ornl.gov
[2] Argonne National Laboratory, Argonne, IL, USA
{zhengchun.liu,kettimut,foster}@anl.gov

Abstract. To support increasingly distributed scientific and big-data applications, powerful data transfer infrastructures are being built with dedicated networks and software frameworks customized to distributed file systems and data transfer nodes. The data transfer performance of such infrastructures critically depends on the combined choices of file, disk, and host systems as well as network protocols and file transfer software, all of which may vary across sites. The randomness of throughput measurements makes it challenging to assess the impact of these choices on the performance of infrastructure or its parts. We propose regression-based throughput profiles by aggregating measurements from sites of the infrastructure, with RTT as the independent variable. The peak values and convex-concave shape of a profile together determine the overall throughput performance of memory and file transfers, and its variations show the performance differences among the sites. We then present projection and difference operators, and coefficients of throughput profiles to characterize the performance of infrastructure and its parts, including sites and file transfer tools. In particular, the utilization-concavity coefficient provides a value in the range $[0, 1]$ that reflects overall transfer effectiveness. We present results of measurements collected using (i) testbed experiments over dedicated 0–366 ms 10 Gbps connections with combinations of TCP versions, file systems, host systems and transfer tools, and (ii) Globus GridFTP transfers over production infrastructure with varying site configurations.

Keywords: Data transfer · Infrastructure · Throughput profile

This work is funded by RAMSES project and the Applied Mathematics Program, Office of Advanced Computing Research, U.S. Department of Energy, and by Extreme Scale Systems Center, sponsored by U. S. Department of Defense, and performed at Oak Ridge National Laboratory managed by UT-Battelle, LLC for U.S. Department of Energy under Contract No. DE-AC05-00OR22725.

1   Introduction

Data transport infrastructures consisting of dedicated network connections, file systems, data transfer nodes, and custom software frameworks are being deployed in scientific and commercial environments. These infrastructures are critical to many High Performance Computing (HPC) scientific workflows, which increasingly demand higher data volumes and sophistication (e.g., streaming, computational monitoring and steering) [21]. The data transfer performance of such infrastructures critically depends on the configuration choices of:

(i)   data transfer host systems, which can vary significantly in terms of number of cores, Network Interface Card (NIC) capability, and connectivity;

(ii) file and disk systems, such as Lustre [22], GPFS [9], and XFS [37] installed on Solid State Disk (SSD) or hard disk arrays;

(iii) network protocols, for example, CUBIC [32], H-TCP [34], and BBR [7] versions of Transmission Control Protocol (TCP); and

(iv) file transfer software such as Globus [4] and GridFTP [3], XDD [33,36], UDT [10], MDTM [25], and Aspera [6], and LNet extensions of Lustre [28].

Our main focus is on workloads with sufficient data volumes to require a close-to-full utilization of the underlying file, IO and network capacities.

Big data and scientific applications are becoming increasingly distributed, and often require coordinated computations at geographically distributed sites that require access to memory data and files over Wide-Area Networks (WANs) [16,21]. Memory transfers are supported by TCP, with performance depending on its version and parameters such as buffer size and number of parallel streams. For example, Data Transfer Nodes (DTNs) used in the U. S. Department of Energy (DOE) infrastructure typically employ H-TCP and buffer sizes recommended for 200 ms Round Trip Time (RTT), and use Globus [4] to drive multiple streams for a single transfer. Typically, file systems are installed at local sites, and wide-area file transfers are carried out by using transfer frameworks [8], mounting file systems over WAN [13,26], and extending IB Lustre to WAN using LNet routers [28]. In this paper, we specifically consider file transfers over shared and dedicated connections, such as those provisioned by ESnet's OSCARS [27] and Google's Software Defined Network (SDN) [15], and use TCP for underlying data transport. In our infrastructures, site DTNs and file system vary significantly but H-TCP and Globus are dominant options.

The transport performance of an infrastructure S is characterized by its *throughput profile* $\hat{\Theta}_A^S(\tau)$ over connections of RTT τ, where the modality $A = T$ corresponds to memory-to-memory transfers using TCP and $A = E$ to disk-to-disk file transfers. Such a profile is generated by aggregating throughput measurements over site connections, and is extrapolated and interpolated to other values of τ using regression or machine learning methods. It captures the combined effects of various sites, components and their configurations; in particular, for file transfers, it reflects the composition effects of file systems, network connections and their couplings through buffer management, which vary significantly across the sites of production infrastructures studied here.

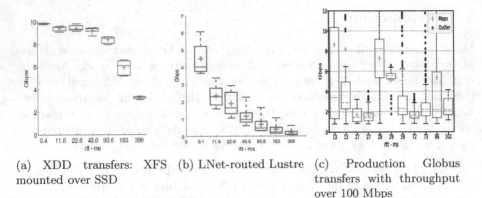

(a) XDD transfers: XFS mounted over SSD

(b) LNet-routed Lustre

(c) Production Globus transfers with throughput over 100 Mbps

Fig. 1. Measurements used for throughput profiles $\hat{\Theta}_E$ of file transfers. The concave profile in near-optimal case of XDD transfers in (a) and the convex profile in (b) due to LNet router limits are both discernable. For Globus transfers over production infrastructure, the site differences lead to larger variations with respect to RTT.

Consider three scenarios: (a) XDD transfers between identical testbed sites with XFS file systems mounted on SSD storage, (b) file copies between identical sites with Lustre file systems extended with LNet routers, and (c) Globus transfers between various pairs of DOE production sites, each with its own WAN connectivity, local network architectures, network interfaces, file system (e.g., Lustre or GPFS), and storage system. In the first two cases, communications occur over dedicated 10GigE connections, for $\tau \in [0, 366]$ ms; in the third case, they are over the production ESnet infrastructure with $\tau \in [0, 105]$ ms. Figures 1a–c show profiles for these three scenarios. We observe that the two profiles over dedicated connections, (a) and (b), are quite different in their peak throughputs (10 and 4.5 Gbps) and their *concave* and *convex* shapes, respectively. While peak throughput is a direct indicator of performance, the concave-convex geometry is a more subtle indicator [18,29]: a concave (convex) profile indicates intermediate-RTT throughput higher (lower) than linear interpolations. The third profile, (c), in contrast, is highly non-smooth, where each point represents measurements between a pair of DOE sites. From an infrastructure throughput perspective, a smooth and concave profile similar to Fig. 1a is desired, which is achieved by (i) enhancing and optimizing sites so that their profiles closely match, thereby making the infrastructure profile smooth, and (ii) selecting TCP version and transport method parameters to make the profile as concave as possible.

We present operators and coefficients of profiles for a part or version $\mathcal{S}'$ of infrastructure $\mathcal{S}$ to assess its component combinations:

– *Profile Calculus*: The projection and difference operators provide profiles $\Theta_A^{\mathcal{S}'}$ corresponding to individual sites and their collections, and to the separate contributions of TCP and file transfer tools.

– *Performance Coefficients*: Coefficients of a profile $\Theta_A^{S'}$ capture the overall utilization and the extent of concavity-convexity, and the combined overall effects of those two elements.

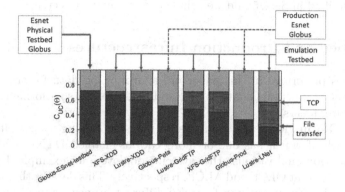

Fig. 2. Summary of $\mathcal{C}_{UC}$ for eight file transfer configurations. In each case, the lower (blue) region is measured disk-to-disk performance; the middle (green) region is additional throughput achieved by TCP memory transfers (when measurements are available); and the upper (yellow) region is network capacity not used by transfers. (Color figure online)

We propose the *utilization-concavity coefficient* $\mathcal{C}_{UC} \in [0,1]$, a scalar metric that captures both the peak throughput and the concave region of $\hat{\Theta}_A^{S'}(\tau)$, and thus enables an objective comparison of different versions S' of S. By combining the profiles and coefficients of throughput measurements from testbeds and production deployments, we analyze the performance of data transfer infrastructures in terms of current and newer components. A summary of our analytics is illustrated in Fig. 2 with $\mathcal{C}_{UC}$ for eight different file transfer configurations, wherein the performance decreases from left to right. The two left-most bars are for Globus transfers over the ESnet testbed DTNs for 0–150 ms connections, and XDD transfers over dedicated, emulated 0–366 ms connections (data from Fig. 1a). They represent near-optimal configurations. The right-most bar represents the worst case corresponding to Lustre LNet transfers over emulated infrastructure (data from Fig. 1b). The performance of Globus transfers over production infrastructure lies in between but below 0.5, indicating potential for site improvements reflected by $\mathcal{C}_{UC}$'s of individual sites in Sect. 4.2. In general our analytics lead to the selection and performance optimizations of various sites and parts of the infrastructure. These measurements have been collected over a five-year period to cover various testbed configurations and log production transfers; individual $\mathcal{C}_{UC}$ computations typically use 10 measurements at each RTT collected within a few hours. In this paper, we only present summaries that highlight the significant roles of (i) individual sites and sub-infrastructures, (ii) buffer sizes, IO limits and parallelism in TCP, GridFTP, XDD and LNet routers, and (iii) TCP versions and file transfer methods and their parameters.

The organization of this paper is as follows. Testbed and Globus infrastructure used for measurements are described in Sect. 2. In Sect. 3, we present throughput profiles for various scenarios, and describe their operators and coefficients. Throughput measurements and analytics are presented in Sect. 4. Related work is described in Sect. 5 and we conclude the paper in Sect. 6.

2   Testbed and Production Infrastructures

The analyses performed in this paper use a mix of log data for transfers performed by the production Globus service and measurements performed in various testbed environments.

For the **Globus log data**, we focus on transfers among the six sites shown in Fig. 3, each of which has one or more Globus-enabled DTNs, a high-speed ESnet connection, and various other systems deployed, for example, Lustre and GPFS file systems at OLCF and ALCF, respectively. This dataset thus comprises performance data for many transfers with different properties (e.g., number and size of files) and end system types, performed at different times.

To enable more controlled studies in a similar environment, we also perform experiments on an **emulation testbed** at ORNL comprising 32-core (feyn1–feyn4, tait1, tait2) and 48-core (bohr05, bohr06) Linux workstations, QDR IB switches, and 10 Gbps hardware connection emulators. We conduct experiments in which hosts with identical configurations are connected in pairs while RTT is varied from 0 to 366 ms. We include the 366 ms RTT case to represent a connection spanning the globe, as a limiting case. We perform memory-to-memory TCP throughput measurements with *iperf* [14] and measure the performance of other transfer tools by running them on the end system computers. Typically, we use 1–10 parallel streams for each configuration, set TCP buffer sizes to the largest value allowed by the host kernel to avoid TCP-level performance bottlenecks (resulting in the allocation of 2 GB socket buffers for iperf), and repeat throughput measurements 10 times. The emulation testbed also includes a distributed Lustre file system supported by eight OSTs connected over an IB QDR switch. Host systems (bohr*, tait*) are connected to the IB switch via Host Channel Adapter (HCA) and to Ethernet via 10 Gbps Ethernet NICs. In addition, our SSD drives are connected over PCI buses on bohr05 and bohr06, which mount local XFS file systems. We also consider configurations in which Lustre is mounted over long-haul connections using LNet routers on tait1 and bohr06; in that case, we use IOzone [1] for throughput measurements for both site and remote file systems.

We also study a **petascale DTN network** comprising the Globus endpoints and associated DTNs at ALCF, the National Center for Supercomputing Applications (NCSA), NERSC, and OLCF. As shown in Table 1, these endpoints differ in their configurations, but each operates multiple DTNs (compute systems dedicated for data transfers in distributed science environments [20]) to enable high-speed data transfers and all are connected at 100 Gbps. We conduct experiments on the petascale DTN network transferring a portion of a real

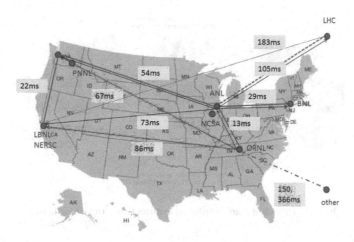

Fig. 3. File transfer infrastructure, showing the six Globus sites and their connections, in blue, plus other connections (in red) considered in emulation studies. The sites are the Argonne Leadership Computing Facility (ALCF) at Argonne National Laboratory (ANL), Brookhaven National Laboratory (BNL), National Energy Research Scientific Computing Center (NERSC) at Lawrence Berkeley National Laboratory (LBNL), Pacific Northwest National Laboratory (PNNL), Oak Ridge Leadership Computing Facility (OLCF) at Oak Ridge National Laboratory (ORNL), and Large Hadron Collider (LHC) at CERN in Europe.

science data generated by cosmology simulations [11]. The dataset consists of 19,260 files totaling 4.4 TB, with file sizes ranging from 1 byte to 11 GB.

Finally, we conduct experiments between the **ESnet testbed data transfer nodes** [2] attached to the production production ESnet network. These DTNs are deployed at NERSC, Chicago, New York and CERN, and are primarily intended for performance testing. Together, these testbed and production infrastructures provide flexible configurations under which various combinations of file systems, TCP versions, XDD, and GridFTP, and their parameters can be assessed. The many combinations resulted in the collection of several Terabytes of measurements data, which we analyze in this paper.

Table 1. Network configurations at the four petascale DTN network sites. All have 100 Gbps WAN connectivity

Institution	ALCF	NCSA	NERSC	OLCF
No. of DTNs	12	23	9	8
Filesystem	GPFS	Lustre	GPFS	Lustre

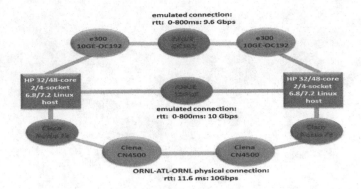

Fig. 4. Physical and emulated connections between hosts

3   Profiles and Coefficients

We consider an infrastructure $\mathcal{S} = \{S_1, S_2, \ldots, S_N\}$, where each site S_i comprises file system F_i and transfer host H_i, and is connected to other sites $S_j, j \neq i$. For example, $N = 7$ for the emulation scenario with sites, ANL, BNL, NERSC, PNL, ORNL, CERN and round-the-earth site, in Fig. 3. Let $\mathcal{S}_{\tau_i}$ denote the set of RTTs of connections used by site S_i to support transfers, and $\mathcal{S}_\tau$ is set of all connections of all sites of $\mathcal{S}$. The *throughput profile* $\hat{\Theta}_A^{\mathcal{S}}(\tau)$ is generated by using measurements at selected RTT $\tau_{i,j} \in \mathcal{S}_\tau$ between sites S_i and S_j and "extended" to other τ, for example, using measurements to additional client sites and computational methods such as piece-wise linear extrapolation. This concept generalizes the throughput profiles to infrastructures with multiple sites from its previous use for single client-server connections [31].

3.1   Variety of Throughput Profiles

The throughput profile $\hat{\Theta}_A^{\mathcal{S}}(\tau)$ is a complex composition of profiles of host and file systems, TCP over network connections, and file transfer software, which may vary across the sites due to their choices and configurations.

Host and File IO Profiles. IO profiles of distributed Lustre and GPFS file systems at OLCF and ALCF with peak write rates of 12 and 60 Gbps, are shown in Figs. 5a and b, respectively. Such variations in peak rates will be reflected in file transfer throughput over connections with these file systems as end points, typically through complex relationships based on the underlying rate limiting factors. When limited by disk or HCA speeds, they represent peak file transfer throughput which is not improved by parallel streams; in particular, they expose throughput limits for large transfers that exceed the host buffers, since in some cases smaller transfers are handled between buffers at a higher throughput. On the other hand, they represent per-process limits in the case of distributed file

systems such as Lustre. File transfer throughput then can be improved significantly by multiple stripes and parallel streams, for example by using higher CC
(number of files transferred concurrently) and P (number of TCP streams per
file) parameters [20], respectively, for GridFTP.

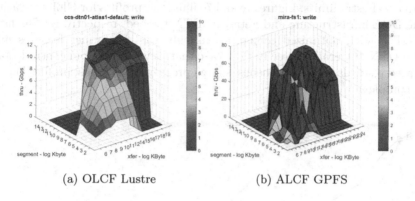

(a) OLCF Lustre   (b) ALCF GPFS

Fig. 5. Throughput profiles of four file systems used in our experiments

TCP Profiles. We show throughput profiles for CUBIC, H-TCP, and BBR
in Fig. 6 for largest allowed buffer sizes on the hosts that are connected by
SONET connections. In all cases, more streams lead to higher throughput, and
H-TCP, which is currently deployed in DTNs, performs better than CUBIC
(Linux default). Recently developed BBR outperforms others with less than 5%
decrease in parallel throughput for 366 ms connections, compared to more than
10% decrease of H-TCP.

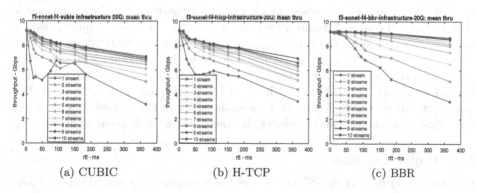

(a) CUBIC   (b) H-TCP   (c) BBR

Fig. 6. Throughput profiles for four TCP versions between **feyn3** and **feyn4** over
SONET

File Transfer Profiles. File transfer profiles vary significantly based on the file systems at source and destination and the transfer tool used to move data between sites. Transfer performance using XDD matches TCP throughput with the XFS file system on SSD, as shown in Fig. 7a, whereas GridFTP transfers between Lustre and XFS achieve much lower throughput, as shown in Fig. 7b, in part due to Lustre limits. Figures 1c and 7c illustrate profiles for Globus transfers on the DOE infrastructure and Petascale DTN testbed, respectively. The latter uses DTNs with optimized configurations, whereas the former features more diverse DTNs. Overall, we see in Figs. 7a–c that as we move from controlled and dedicated testbeds to heterogeneous, shared production systems, profiles become more complex.

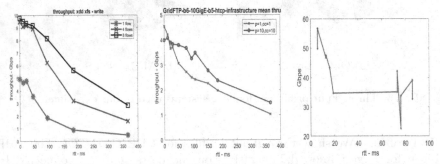

(a) XDD on XFS with SSD(b) GridFTP: Lustre – XFS(c) Petascale DTN testbed transfers

Fig. 7. Throughput profiles of file transfers.

The infrastructure profiles show significant variations and complex dependencies on the component systems, which motivates the need for simple measures that capture the overall performance, even if further analysis requires deeper investigations. Despite the variability, these profiles also satisfy important stability properties with respect to RTT in emulations in that profiles of its smaller subsets provide reasonable approximations; as illustrated in Fig. 8, a profile with five RTTs is within 2% of that with 11 RTTs. Consequently, we choose smaller representative sets of RTTs out of 28 possible values in the analysis of emulation scenarios, which significantly reduces the measurement collection time.

3.2   Profile Calculus

Consider an infrastructure S' whose sites have the same configurations as those of S, for example, its sub-infrastructure. The *projection operator* $\mathcal{R}$, generates throughput values for S'_τ, given those for S_τ such that $\mathcal{R}\left(\hat{\Theta}^S, S'\right) = \hat{\Theta}^{S'}$. This operator can be used to infer a profile for an individual site in S, $\hat{\Theta}^{S_i} = \hat{\Theta}^{\{S_i\}}$, and also for a future site S_C of S as $\hat{\Theta}^{\{S_C\}}$ based on the RTTs of the new site's connections.

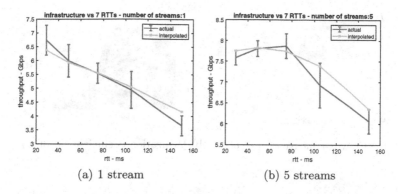

(a) 1 stream   (b) 5 streams

Fig. 8. Profiles constructed from measurements performed on the `bohr5–10GigE–bohr6` emulation testbed at 11 RTT values (blue lines, with error bars) vs. profiles constructed from measurements at just five RTT values (red lines). (Color figure online)

We define the *difference operator* for two profiles $\hat{\Theta}_1$ and $\hat{\Theta}_2$ as $\left(\hat{\Theta}_1 \ominus \hat{\Theta}_2\right)(\tau) = \hat{\Theta}_1(\tau) - \hat{\Theta}_2(\tau)$. By using different profiles, this operator can be used to provide, for example, an incremental profile of a file transfer tool, F, as $\Theta_F = \Theta_{E|T} = \hat{\Theta}_T \ominus \hat{\Theta}_E$. When used with $\hat{\Theta}_T$ for different TCP versions, it characterizes the effectiveness of file transfer tool F under a given TCP version. In ideal cases, $\Theta_{E|T}$ is close to the zero function as in the case of XDD transfers using XFS on SSD as shown in Fig. 7a.

3.3 Utilization and Convex-Concave Coefficients

Let L represent the connection capacity, and τ_L and τ_H denote the smallest and largest RTTs, respectively, of the infrastructure. Then, we define the *under utilization coefficient* of $\hat{\Theta}$ as $\mathcal{C}_U(\hat{\Theta}) = \int_{\tau_L}^{\tau_R} \left(L - \hat{\Theta}(\tau)\right) d\tau$. By applying to memory and file transfer throughput, we have $\mathcal{C}_U(\hat{\Theta}_T)$ and $\mathcal{C}_U(\hat{\Theta}_E)$ that represent the unused connection capacity by TCP and the file transfer method, respectively, as shown in Fig. 2 for emulation testbed configurations. Then, the file transfer method $\mathcal{C}_U(\hat{\Theta}_T \ominus \hat{\Theta}_E)$ captures its effectiveness by using TCP profile as a baseline.

The convex and concave properties of $\hat{\Theta}$ are specified by the area above and below the linear interpolation of $\hat{\Theta}(\tau_L)$ and $\hat{\Theta}(\tau_R)$, respectively. This area is positive for a concave profile and negative for a convex profile. We define this area as the *convex-concave coefficient* of $\hat{\Theta}$, as illustrated in Fig. 9a, and it is given by

$$\mathcal{C}_{CC}\left(\hat{\Theta}\right) = \int_{\tau_L}^{\tau_R} \left(\hat{\Theta}(\tau) - \left[\hat{\Theta}(\tau_L) + \frac{\hat{\Theta}(\tau_R) - \hat{\Theta}(\tau_L)}{\tau_R - \tau_L}\tau\right]\right) d\tau$$

$$= (\tau_R - \tau_L)\left[\bar{\hat{\Theta}} - \hat{\Theta}_M\right].$$

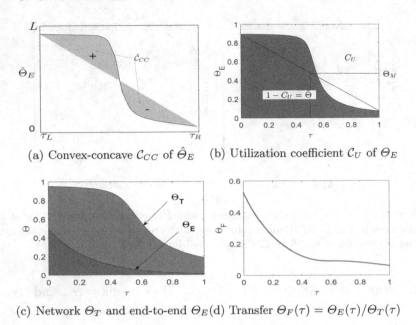

(a) Convex-concave $\mathcal{C}_{CC}$ of $\hat{\Theta}_E$ (b) Utilization coefficient $\mathcal{C}_U$ of Θ_E

(c) Network Θ_T and end-to-end Θ_E(d) Transfer $\Theta_F(\tau) = \Theta_E(\tau)/\Theta_T(\tau)$

Fig. 9. Throughput profiles and coefficients

Let $\tilde{\Theta} : [0,1] \mapsto [0,1]$ denote a normalized version of $\hat{\Theta}$ such that throughput values are scaled by L, and the operand τ is translated and scaled from interval $[\tau_L, \tau_R]$ to $[0,1]$. We now combine both utilization and convex-concave properties and define the *utilization-concavity coefficient* as

$$\mathcal{C}_{UC}\left(\hat{\Theta}\right) = \frac{1}{2}\left(\left[1 - \mathcal{C}_U\left(\tilde{\Theta}\right)\right] + \left[\frac{1}{2} + \mathcal{C}_{CC}\left(\tilde{\Theta}\right)\right]\right).$$

It takes a much simpler form $\mathcal{C}_{UC}\left(\hat{\Theta}\right) = \bar{\tilde{\Theta}} - \tilde{\Theta}_M/2 + 1/4$ such that $\bar{\tilde{\Theta}}$ is the average and $\tilde{\Theta}_M/2$ is throughput at midpoint, which are closely related. The variations with respect to RTT in profiles, as observed in production Globus transfers infrastructures in Fig. 1c, lead to lower $\bar{\tilde{\Theta}}$ and hence lower $\mathcal{C}_{UC}$. These variations are due to differences in site systems which lead to lower $\mathcal{C}_{UC}$ compared to smoother emulation profiles of infrastructures with identical host systems in Fig. 7a, namely, all with XFS on SSD. However, smoother profiles can also be achieved for transfers between distributed Lustre and XFS on single SSD device as shown in Fig. 7b for CC = 10 for GridFTP.

3.4   File Transfer Method Profiles

Let us assume that we have performed performance measurements for both memory-to-memory and disk-to-disk transfers over some infrastructure, and normalized the results to [0, 1]. We may see something like the network profile $\tilde{\Theta}_T(\tau)$

and file transfer profile $\tilde{\Theta}_E(\tau)$ shown in Fig. 9c. The gap between the two profiles illustrates the effects of the file system, storage system, and file transfer method. Since $\tilde{\Theta}_E(\tau)$ encompasses TCP profile $\Theta_T(\tau)$ and host file IO limits, its lower values may be due to file IO throughput limits and not necessarily due to how well the transfer method, for example, manages IO-network transfer buffers. In particular, lower values of $\tilde{\Theta}_E(\tau)$ could be due to lower file IO throughput of the file system $\hat{\Theta}_{F_i}$ and/or host system $\hat{\Theta}_{H_i}$ at site S_i. We can assess the performance of the file transfer method F itself by suitably normalizing with respect to the site profiles. If site throughputs are higher, we define the throughput profile of the file transfer part as $\hat{\Theta}_F(\tau) = \tilde{\Theta}_E(\tau)/\tilde{\Theta}_T(\tau)$, for $\tau \in [0, 1]$, as illustrated in Fig. 9d. We consider that TCP profile is a non-increasing function of τ. When file or host system at a site limits TCP throughput most among the sites such that $\min\{\hat{\Theta}_{H_i}, \hat{\Theta}_{F_i}\} < \hat{\Theta}_T(0)$, we define

$$\tilde{\Theta}_F(\tau) = \frac{\tilde{\Theta}_E(\tau) L}{\tilde{\Theta}_T(\tau) \min\{\hat{\Theta}_{H_i}, \hat{\Theta}_{F_i}\}}, \tag{2.2}$$

for $\tau \in [0, 1]$. Then, the utilization-concavity coefficient of the file transfer part is given by $\mathcal{C}_{UC}\left(\hat{\Theta}_F\right)$.

4   Throughput Profiles and Analytics

Production deployments of data transfer infrastructure spanning multiple sites could be quite heterogeneous; for example, DOE infrastructure employs different file systems (Lustre and GPFS), protocols (H-TCP on DTNs and CUBIC on cluster nodes), network connections (10GigE nd 40GigE) and file transfer software (GridFTP, bbcp and others). The projection and difference operations enable us to extract the profiles and coefficients of parts of the infrastructure its profile estimated from measurements. However, they are limited to the existing components, and assessment of other, in particular, newer components is not practical since the sites are independently operated and maintained. Our approach combines emulations, testbeds, and production infrastructures to support these tasks. We use four types of resources to generate datasets that drive the analytics, as described in Sect. 2.

The emulation testbed enables broad and flexible configurations but only a limited reflection of production aspects. In contrast, Globus measurements provide a true reflection of production transfers, but offer limited scope for testing potentially disruptive technologies such as LNet-routed Lustre system. The ESnet DTNs offers more flexible configurations but its connections are limited by its much smaller footprint, and it does not support cluster nodes and Lustre file system. The Petascale experiments are constrained by the site systems and footprint of current infrastructure but offers several optimizations to select DTNs. By combining results from all four systems, we gain new insights into current and future data infrastructures, as discussed subsequently in this section.

4.1   Testbed Measurements

The dedicated ORNL testbed and its support for Lustre and for XFS on SSD enables us to test specialized scenarios such as BBR-enabled infrastructure, LNet-based wide-area extensions of Lustre, and data transfers between DTN-class hosts and cluster nodes.

Site Profiles. The $\mathcal{C}_{UC}$ values for TCP and GridFTP file transfer throughput for the `bohr5-10GigE-bohr6` configuration with H-TCP and 10 parallel streams are shown in Figs. 10a and b respectively. In addition to infrastructure profiles (labeled "all"), we also extract site-specific transfer throughput performance (i.e., transfers to/from a particular site) for ANL, ORNL, and LBNL, and show their individual $\mathcal{C}_{UC}$ values in these figures. We now focus on GridFTP software component at each site. The normalized filesystem throughput profile, namely, the ratio of the end-to-end file transfer and iperf throughput in Eq. (2.2), characterizes the performance of GridFTP specific to sites, and their $\mathcal{C}_{UC}(\hat{\Theta}_F)$ plots are shown in Fig. 10c. We see that these individual site $\mathcal{C}_{UC}$ curves closely match the infrastructure curve in all three cases, which is an artifact of the site systems being similar in the testbed.

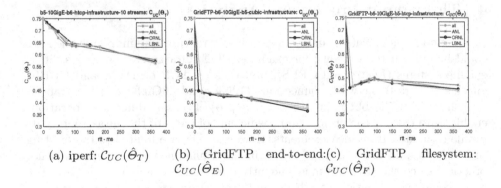

(a) iperf: $\mathcal{C}_{UC}(\hat{\Theta}_T)$ (b) GridFTP end-to-end:(c) GridFTP filesystem:
$\mathcal{C}_{UC}(\hat{\Theta}_E)$ $\mathcal{C}_{UC}(\hat{\Theta}_F)$

Fig. 10. $\mathcal{C}_{UC}$ plots for `bohr5-10GigE-bohr6` configuration with H-TCP and 10 parallel streams: Overall and site profiles

File Transfers. We consider transfers similar to those plotted in Fig. 7a but with Lustre filesystem, where two stripes are used for default and direct IO options. Figure 11 plots the $\mathcal{C}_{UC}(\hat{\Theta}_E)$ values for both options with 1, 4, and 8 flows. It is interesting to note that while for direct IO Lustre, the transfer performance improves with higher flow counts, as evidenced by the higher $\mathcal{C}_{UC}(\hat{\Theta}_E)$ curves, the default IO Lustre option does not share the same characteristics: using 4 flows yields the best performance, which has also been observed in [30].

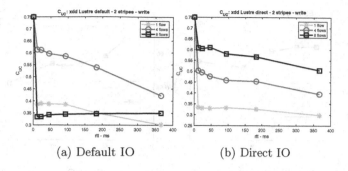

(a) Default IO (b) Direct IO

Fig. 11. $\mathcal{C}_{UC}(\hat{\Theta}_E)$ for XDD transfers with two stripes and direct IO Lustre

Finally, we plot $\mathcal{C}_{UC}$ of profiles for TCP, end-to-end transfer, and file transfer mechanism for eight-stripe LNet Lustre configuration in Fig. 12. The underlying LNet file transfer mechanism is significantly different from GridFTP and XDD software, and its throughput is limited by LNet peer credits which in turn results in lower and more convex profile compared to the above XDD cases. Indeed, the $\mathcal{C}_{UC}(\hat{\Theta}_E)$ values are lower and drop to below 0.4 even at lower RTTs, reflecting the inferior LNet performance. Here, $\mathcal{C}_{UC}(\hat{\Theta}_F)$ for LNet component is obtained using the difference operator, which shows the use of calculus to estimate its effect on infrastructure throughput, as discussed in Sect. 3.4.

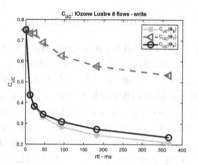

Fig. 12. $\mathcal{C}_{UC}$ values for measurements of Lustre file copies

ESNet DTNs. For ESnet testbed, we consider Globus file transfers among DTNs located at four sites. We vary both the concurrency CC and parallelism P values within $\{1, 2, 4, 8, 16\}$ with a total of 25 possible CC and P combinations for each of the 16 connections. Figure 13a shows throughput profiles for four selected configurations with smallest and largest CC and P values. The configuration with $CC = 1$ exhibits much reduced throughput compared to that with $CC = 16$, whereas in the former case, using $P = 16$ leads to significantly higher throughput compared to using $P = 1$, especially for higher RTTs. The $\mathcal{C}_{UC}(\hat{\Theta}_E)$ plots in Fig. 13b also show a superior performance with higher CC values, as evidenced by the nearly level $\mathcal{C}_{UC}$ values with increasing RTT, in stark contrast to the precipitous drop in $\mathcal{C}_{UC}$ when $CC = P = 1$.

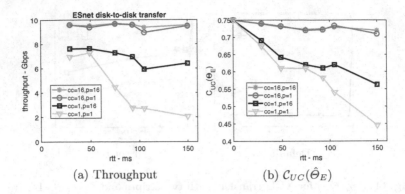

(a) Throughput   (b) $\mathcal{C}_{UC}(\hat{\Theta}_E)$

Fig. 13. ESnet testbed DTNs: Globus file transfer throughput and corresponding $\mathcal{C}_{UC}(\hat{\Theta}_E)$ profiles for different concurrency (CC) and parallelism (P) values.

4.2 Globus Measurements

We processed Globus logs from the four Petascale DTN sites to obtain throughput profiles, and computed $\mathcal{C}_{UC}$ values in Fig. 14(c) with 100 Gbps network capacity. The profiles of individual sites are shown in Fig. 14a, whose profiles differ both in peak throughput and rate of decrease; they all have convex profiles with $\mathcal{C}_{UC}$ values below 0.5. The infrastructure profile shown in Fig. 7c interestingly has a higher $\mathcal{C}_{UC}$ value compared to the sites. The convexity of these profiles indicates that network flows have not reach their full rates and indeed the throughput is limited by site IO or file systems). Among the four sites, ANL and ORNL have file systems with the highest measured throughput (Fig. 5), and the profile of ANL-ORNL sub-infrastructure is shown in Fig. 14b; although still convex, its profile is smoother and its $\mathcal{C}_{UC}$ is higher than that of both sites.

The second set of Global logs are collected over ESnet production infrastructure for a wide variety of transfers that included DTNs and other servers from five sites ANL, BNL, NERSC, PNNL, and ORNL. Our interest is mainly in high transfer rates, and we computed profiles using transfers with rates of at least 100 Mbps as shown in Fig. 15. Unlike the previous case, not all servers have been configured for high throughput, which resulted in a wide range of site profiles shown in Fig. 15a. To account for them in computing $\mathcal{C}_{UC}$, we use a lower connection capacity of 10 Gbps. This profile of the infrastructure with five sites is much more complex than its counterpart in testbed measurements, reflecting the more varied nature of site configurations; however, the overall profile decreases with RTT and is convex as indicated by $\mathcal{C}_{UC} = 0.343$. Among the sites, ANL and ORNL achieve higher throughput and contain concave regions as reflected by their $\mathcal{C}_{UC}$ values above 0.5. However, the profile of ANL-ORNL sub-infrastructure has additional concave regions as shown in Fig. 15b, and their combined profile has $\mathcal{C}_{UC} = 0.459$, which is lower than that of either site. Thus, the effect of site profiles on infrastructure profiles is the opposite of the previous case. The overall convexity of profiles indicates potential improvements in throughput by overcoming IO and file throughput limits and also improving the

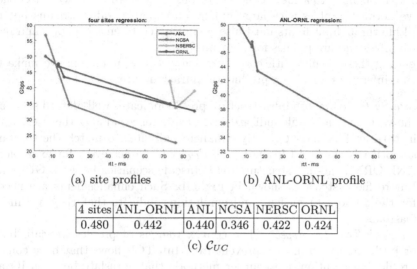

(a) site profiles   (b) ANL-ORNL profile

4 sites	ANL-ORNL	ANL	NCSA	NERSC	ORNL
0.480	0.442	0.440	0.346	0.422	0.424

(c) $\mathcal{C}_{UC}$

Fig. 14. Using Globus transfer log data to characterize 100 Gbps-connected Petascale DTNs at ANL, NCSA, NERSC, and ORNL. (a) Profiles for each site, based on average performance to each other site. (b) An aggregate profile based on just measurements from ANL and ORNL to each other site (including each other). (c) $\mathcal{C}_{UC}$ values for the aggregate of all sites, just the transfers in (b), and each site in (a).

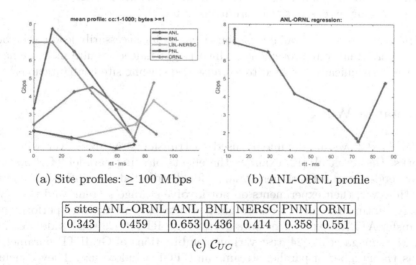

(a) Site profiles: $\geq$ 100 Mbps   (b) ANL-ORNL profile

5 sites	ANL-ORNL	ANL	BNL	NERSC	PNNL	ORNL
0.343	0.459	0.653	0.436	0.414	0.358	0.551

(c) $\mathcal{C}_{UC}$

Fig. 15. Using log data for Globus transfers of $\geq$100 Mbps to characterize 10 Gbps-connected servers at ANL, BNL, NERSC, PNNL and ORNL. See Fig. 14 for a description of each subfigure.

network throughput to achieve concave regions. It is possible to achieve broader concave network profiles with large buffers and more parallel streams but the IO and file throughput limits must also be mitigated to ensure higher and more concave infrastructure profiles for file transfers.

Relating these results with corresponding testbed emulations we make the following inferences about the production infrastructure:

(i) *Site Systems:* Smooth infrastructure profile indicates well-aligned sites, and the variations in profile indicate critical differences among the sites, which in turn lead to lower $\mathcal{C}_{UC}$. By enhancing all sites to match the top ones, smoother profiles and hence higher $\mathcal{C}_{UC}$ will be achieved; for example, in ANL-ORNL sub-infrastructure for Petascale scenarios between GPFS and Lustre file systems as shown in Fig. 14b. Such enhancements are needed for these Globus transfers, and emulations indicate that they are indeed feasible.

(ii) *Network Transfer Aspects:* The convex regions of profiles indicate buffer or IO limits which in turn prevent from full TCP flows that have concave profiles. In addition, file transfer methods that translate between IO and network flows lead to rate or buffer limits that in turn result in convex profiles, which can be overcome by matching parallel IO and TCP flows as illustrated in Fig. 7a with 8 flows. Again, our testbed emulations indicate that these improvements are feasible, for example by using BBR TCP and suitable CC and P values for GridFTP.

(iii) *Measurements:* The profiles and corresponding $\mathcal{C}_{UC}$ values are generated from Globus logs of transfers which are collected non-intrusively. They provide the above valuable information about sites and network transfers without needing extensive site instrumentation.

The inferences based on available Globus logs do not necessarily lead to the best possible performance improvements, which might indeed require measurements of transfers specifically designed to exercise the specific site configurations.

5   Related Work

Parallel TCP flows are commonly used to transfer large data over wide-area networks. Hacker et al. [12] examine the effects of using parallel TCP flows to improve end-to-end network performance for distributed data-intensive applications. However, their experiments do not involve storage systems and thus only partially capture the factors determining end-to-end file transfer performance. To transfer ATLAS experiment data over a high RTT ($\sim$290 ms) wide area network, Matsunaga et al. [24] test various combinations of GridFTP parameters, such as the number of parallel streams and TCP window size. They conclude that careful parameter optimization is needed for bulk data transfer, especially over high-RTT networks because default configurations are usually optimized for short RTTs and large RTTs lead to quite different behavior. Kosar et al. have also investigated the impact of such parameters and developed automated parameter selection methods [5,38,39]. In a different take on the modeling problem, Liu et al. [21] introduce methods for evaluating potential design points of a distributed multi-site infrastructure. Their use case demonstrates the benefits of building such an infrastructure, as well as the requirements of profiling it for better estimation of end-to-end data movement performance.

A complete understanding of a distributed infrastructure requires explanations for each individual subsystem and their interactions. Liu et al. [19] extract features for endpoint CPU load, NIC load and transfer characteristics, and use these features in linear and nonlinear transfer performance models. Some studies have focused on profiling of subsystems [18,29,30] including network, IO, and host systems. In particular, both Rao et al. [29] and Liu et al. [18] have investigated conditions under which the overall memory transfer throughput profile exhibits the desirable concave characteristic, whereas in Rao et al. [30] extensive XDD file transfer throughput performance is discussed. This paper extends the above concavity-convexity analysis to infrastructure data transfers for the first time, whose variations across sites lead to non-smooth profiles. These findings are important: although over the decades, several detailed analytical models have been developed and experimental measurements have been collected for various network transport protocols, e.g., several TCP variants, these conventional models [23,35] provide entirely convex throughput profiles. Thus, they underestimate the throughput, and furthermore do not accurately reflect the superior TCP performance over linear interpolations, at least for smaller RTTs. Liu and Rao [17] apply similar metrics to describe memory data transfer performance for client-server connections using a suite of transport protocols but not to much more complex infrastructure-level file transfers.

For data transfer infrastructures, we know of no reliable analytical methods in the literature for characterizing the data transfer performance for bottleneck detection and accurate performance prediction. Largely motivated by recent proliferation of high-performance distributed computing and networking in scientific and commercial applications, this is our first attempt at filling the void in characterizing data transfer performance by using a single metric applicable to disparate infrastructures to compare them, and to the sites and file transfer mechanisms to pinpoint parts to be improved.

6 Conclusions

We have presented analytics of throughput measurements of wide-area data transfer infrastructures that support science and big data distributed computations. These measurements include both testbed and production infrastructures with the GridFTP and XDD file transfer tools, and the Lustre file system extended with LNet routers. The throughput measurements were quite varied due to the complexities of host, file, IO, and disk systems, and their interactions, which makes performance assessment and optimization of infrastructures or their parts challenging. We presented unifying analytics based on the convexity-concavity geometry of throughput regression profiles, and proposed the utilization-concavity coefficient that characterizes the overall transfer performance as a scalar in [0,1] range. The profiles and their coefficients extracted using measurements from structured testbeds and production infrastructures provide a high-level, summary performance assessment and also indicate potential areas for further deeper investigations. Our results also provided guidelines for performance optimizations by highlighting the significant roles of individual site configurations, and buffer sizes and utilization, and parallelism implemented by network protocols and file transfer methods.

Further investigations, including additional test configurations and examination of additional parameters, are needed to further improve throughput performance over shared connections. In addition to throughput considered here, other parameters and derived quantities may be studied for objective performance comparisons of varied configurations. Of particular importance are the quantities that indicate the levels of optimizations of a given configuration and provide insights for further investigations. It would be of future interest to extend the calculus of throughput profiles described here with a deeper focus on subsystems and broader aspects to encompass data streaming infrastructures.

References

1. Iozone file system benchmark (2018). http://www.iozone.org. Accessed 28 Mar 2018
2. Energy Science Network Data Transfer Nodes. https://fasterdata.es.net/performance-testing/DTNs/. Accessed 28 Mar 2018
3. Allcock, W., et al.: The Globus striped GridFTP framework and server. In: ACM/IEEE Conference on Supercomputing, pp. 54–64. IEEE Computer Society, Washington, D.C. (2005)
4. Allen, B., et al.: Software as a service for data scientists. Commun. ACM **55**(2), 81–88 (2012)
5. Arslan, E., Kosar, T.: High speed transfer optimization based on historical analysis and real-time tuning. IEEE Trans. Parallel Distrib. Syst. **29**, 1303–1316 (2018)
6. Aspera Transfer Service. http://asperasoft.com. Accessed 28 Mar 2018
7. Cardwell, N., Cheng, Y., Gunn, C.S., Yeganeh, S.H., Jacobson, V.: BBR: congestion based congestion control. ACM Queue **14**(5), 50 (2016)
8. Chard, K., Dart, E., Foster, I., Shifflett, D., Tuecke, S.J., Williams, J.: The modern research data portal: a design pattern for networked, data-intensive science. Peer J. Comput. Sci. **4**(6), e144 (2018)
9. General Parallel File System. https://www.ibm.com/support/knowledgecenter/en/SSFKCN/gpfs_welcome.html
10. Gu, Y., Grossman, R.L.: UDT: UDP-based data transfer for high-speed wide area networks. Comput. Netw. **51**(7), 1777–1799 (2007)
11. Habib, S., Morozov, V., Frontiere, N., Finkel, H., Pope, A., Heitmann, K.: HACC: extreme scaling and performance across diverse architectures. In International Conference for High Performance Computing, Networking, Storage and Analysis, SC 2013, pp. 6:1–6:10. ACM, New York (2013)
12. Hacker, T.J., Athey, B.D., Noble, B.: The end-to-end performance effects of parallel TCP sockets on a lossy wide-area network. In: 16th International Parallel and Distributed Processing Symposium (2002)

13. Henschel, R., et al.: Demonstrating Lustre over a 100 Gbps wide area network of 3,500 km. In: International Conference on High Performance Computing, Networking, Storage and Analysis, pp. 1–8, November 2012
14. https://iperf.fr/. iPerf - the ultimate speed test tool for TCP, UDP and SCTPs (2018). https://iperf.fr/. Accessed 28 Mar 2018
15. Jain, S., et al.: B4: experience with a globally-deployed software defined WAN. SIGCOMM Comput. Commun. Rev. **43**(4), 3–14 (2013)
16. Kettimuthu, R., Liu, Z., Wheelerd, D., Foster, I., Heitmann, K., Cappello, F.: Transferring a petabyte in a day. In: 4th International Workshop on Innovating the Network for Data Intensive Science, p. 10, November 2017
17. Liu, Q., Rao, N.S.V.: On concavity and utilization analytics of wide-area network transport protocols. In: Proceedings of the 20th IEEE Conference on High Performance Computing and Communications (HPCC), Exeter, UK, June 2018
18. Liu, Q., Rao, N.S.V., Wu, C.Q., Yun, D., Kettimuthu, R., Foster, I.: Measurement-based performance profiles and dynamics of UDT over dedicated connections. In: International Conference on Network Protocols, Singapore, November 2016
19. Liu, Z., Balaprakash, P., Kettimuthu, R., Foster, I.: Explaining wide area data transfer performance. In: 26th International Symposium on High-Performance Parallel and Distributed Computing, HPDC 2017, pp. 167–178. ACM, New York (2017)
20. Liu, Z., Kettimuthu, R., Foster, I., Beckman, P.H.: Towards a smart data transfer node. In: 4th International Workshop on Innovating the Network for Data Intensive Science, p. 10, November 2017
21. Liu, Z., Kettimuthu, R., Leyffer, S., Palkar, P., Foster, I.: A mathematical programming - and simulation-based framework to evaluate cyberinfrastructure design choices. In: IEEE 13th International Conference on e-Science, p. 148–157, October 2017
22. Lustre Basics. https://www.olcf.ornl.gov/kb_articles/lustre-basics
23. Mathis, M., Semke, J., Mahdavi, J., Ott, T.: The mascroscopic behavior of the TCP congestion avoidance algorithm. Comput. Commun. Rev. **27**(3), 67–82 (1997)
24. Matsunaga, H., Isobe, T., Mashimo, T., Sakamoto, H., Ueda, I.: Data transfer over the wide area network with a large round trip time. J. Phys.: Conf. Ser. **219**(6), 062056 (2010)
25. Multi-core aware data transfer middleware. mdtm.fnal.gov. Accessed 28 Mar 2018
26. Michael, S., Zhen, L., Henschel, R., Simms, S., Barton, E., Link, M.: A study of Lustre networking over a 100 gigabit wide area network with 50 milliseconds of latency. In: 5th International Workshop on Data-Intensive Distributed Computing, pp. 43–52 (2012)
27. On-demand Secure Circuits and Advance Reservation System. http://www.es.net/oscars
28. Rao, N.S.V., Imam, N., Hanley, J., Sarp, O.: Wide-area Lustre file system using LNet routers. In: 12th Annual IEEE International Systems Conference (2018)
29. Rao, N.S.V., et al.: TCP throughput profiles using measurements over dedicated connections. In: ACM Symposium on High-Performance Parallel and Distributed Computing, Washington, D.C., July–August 2017
30. Rao, N.S.V., et al.: Experimental analysis of file transfer rates over wide-area dedicated connections. In: 18th IEEE International Conference on High Performance Computing and Communications (HPCC), Sydney, Australia, pp. 198–205, December 2016

31. Rao, N.S.V., et al.: Experiments and analyses of data transfers over wide-area dedicated connections. In: 26th International Conference on Computer Communications and Network (2017)
32. Rhee, I., Xu, L.: CUBIC: a new TCP-friendly high-speed TCP variant. In: 3rd International Workshop on Protocols for Fast Long-Distance Networks (2005)
33. Settlemyer, B.W., Dobson, J.D., Hodson, S.W., Kuehn, J.A., Poole, S.W., Ruwart, T.M.: A technique for moving large data sets over high-performance long distance networks. In: IEEE 27th Symposium on Mass Storage Systems and Technologies, pp. 1–6, May 2011
34. Shorten, R.N., Leith, D.J.: H-TCP: TCP for high-speed and long-distance networks. In: 3rd International Workshop on Protocols for Fast Long-Distance Networks (2004)
35. Srikant, Y., Ying, L.: Communication Networks: An Optimization, Control, and Stochastic Networks Perspective. Cambridge University Press, Cambridge (2014)
36. XDD - The eXtreme dd toolset. https://github.com/bws/xdd. Accessed 28 Mar 2018
37. XFS. http://xfs.org
38. Yildirim, E., Arslan, E., Kim, J., Kosar, T.: Application-level optimization of big data transfers through pipelining, parallelism and concurrency. IEEE Trans. Cloud Comput. **4**(1), 63–75 (2016)
39. Yildirim, E., Yin, D., Kosar, T.: Prediction of optimal parallelism level in wide area data transfers. IEEE Trans. Parallel Distrib. Syst. **22**(12), 2033–2045 (2011)

Exploring Intelligent Service Migration in Vehicular Networks

Onyekachukwu A. Ezenwigbo[✉], Vishnu Vardhan Paranthaman,
Glenford Mapp, and Ramona Trestian

Faculty of Science and Technology, Middlesex University, London NW4 4BT, UK
{A.Ezenwigbo,V.Paranthaman,G.Mapp,R.Trestian}@mdx.ac.uk

Abstract. Mobile edge clouds have great potential to address the challenges in vehicular networks by transferring storage and computing functions to the cloud. This brings many advantages of the cloud closer to the mobile user, by installing small cloud infrastructures at the network edge. However, it is still a challenge to efficiently utilize heterogeneous communication and edge computing architectures. In this paper, we investigate the impact of live service migration within a Vehicular Ad-hoc Network environment by making use of the results collected from a real experimental test-bed. A new proactive service migration model which considers both the mobility of the user and the service migration time for different services is introduced. Results collected from a real experimental test-bed of connected vehicles show that there is a need to explore proactive service migration based on the mobility of users. This can result in better resource usage and better Quality of Service for the mobile user. Additionally, a study on the performance of the transport protocol and its impact in the context of live service migration for highly mobile environments is presented with results in terms of latency, bandwidth, and burst and their potential effect on the time it takes to migrate services.

Keywords: Edge Computing · Service migration ·
Vehicular Ad-hoc Network · Quality of Service

1 Introduction

Over the years, the cloud-based mobile applications have seen a significant increase in popularity, making it apparent that the next move within the networking arena would be towards an intelligent edge environment. In this context, one of the primary issues is the provision of guaranteed Quality of Service (QoS) for a wide variety of services. The existing centralized structure of the cloud-based architecture has made a general large geographical separation between mobile users and the cloud infrastructure. In this scenario, end-to-end communication between the mobile user and the cloud infrastructure can involve a lot of network hops, thereby introducing high network latency. Additionally, the

© ICST Institute for Computer Sciences, Social Informatics and Telecommunications Engineering 2019
Published by Springer Nature Switzerland AG 2019. All Rights Reserved
H. Gao et al. (Eds.): TridentCom 2018, LNICST 270, pp. 41–61, 2019.
https://doi.org/10.1007/978-3-030-12971-2_3

network bandwidth of the cloud may also depreciate because the cloud infrastructure is accessed on a many-to-one basis [12]. The new approach to resolve the above problems is to install computing infrastructures at the edge of the network.

Technological advances in personal computers, tablets, and smartphones have increased the demand and fabrication of applications and services to support these developments. This has necessitated a rising need for QoS and Quality of Experience(QoE). The processing, memory and storage capacity of these new mobile, portable devices are becoming more industrious but not in terms of supporting high processing application demand within an expected time. These high demanding applications also result in a high level of battery consumption reducing the duration of user device usage. It is on this premise that the Mobile Cloud Computing (MCC) concept was adopted to provide the Mobile Node (MN) with the opportunity of cloud computing [3]. The MCC utilises strong reserved centralized clouds through a core network of a mobile operator and the internet to provide computing and storage facilities to MNs. The MCC is highly beneficial [1] as among other advantages, it helps to offload computing, storage and memory of applications to the cloud which prolongs battery life; allowing the mobile user to access highly developed and demanding applications; as well as making increased storage facilities available to users. However, the traditional cloud for mobile users results in high latency since data is sent to a central cloud sever that is remotely located from its users in terms of network topology.

Furthermore, Edge Computing (EC) is an existing and capable approach to access large data locally and evade extensive latency [19,23], especially in vehicular networks as the MN moves at a high speed and hence, requires low latency. Vehicular users requesting services through a core network from edge networks far from the cloud may cause extensive latency. The EC is established to overcome these disadvantages of traditional cloud computing [17,22]. A lot of research have motivated Vehicular Edge Computing (VEC). Most of the recent research focused on the VEC architecture design still fail to look into mobility and how it can affect service migration in a highly mobile environment.

Moreover, the migration of the cloud services close to MNs helps to address the problem of high latency by moving services close to the MNs, i.e., to the edge of mobile network as considered in newly emerging EC paradigm as part of MCC. However, in the conventional MCC, the cloud services are called up via the Internet connection [16] whereas in the case of the EC, the computing resources are located in proximity of the MNs. Therefore, the EC can offer significantly lower latencies and jitter when compared to the traditional MCC. On the other hand, the EC provides only limited computational and storage resources with respect to the centralised cloud computing.

The Vehicular Ad-Hoc Networks (VANETs) have emerged as a promising field of development and research, VANETs will enable the communication between vehicles and infrastructures on the road to provide services such safety, entertainment and infotainment. In VANET, vehicles and RSUs (Road-Side Units), i.e. network nodes, will be equipped with on-board computation and communication modules to make sure better communication is possible between them. It supports 802.11p which is required to support Intelligent Transportation Systems (ITS) applications because of available high bandwidth [4,15]. Existing research on VANET focuses on communication between end nodes and the infrastructure and hence has failed to look into end to end communication with required QoS and security. Service migration is a technique which can helps in gaining high QoS and QoE by migrating the services closer to the user. Due to the high rate of vehicular mobility in a VANET environment, the highly dynamic topologies are frequently prone to network disconnection and fragmentation. Consequently, these inherent characteristics are bound to degrade the QoS provided by the VANET infrastructures. Therefore, the establishment of robust VANETs that could effectively support applications and services on a large geographical scale remains an open challenge.

There are lots of research efforts that look into migrating the services from the core cloud to the edge of the network but the focus of this paper is to explore service migration between nodes at the edge of the network in order to provide better QoS in vehicular networks. In this context, this paper investigates the benefits of integrating Mobile Edge Computing (MEC) within the Vehicular Ad-Hoc Network (VANET) scenario. A real experimental vehicular network test-bed is introduced. Results collected from this test-bed are used to better understand the impact of live service migration within a VANET environment.

The rest of the paper is structured as follows. Section 2 introduces the literature review while Sect. 3 looks at service delivery for mobile clients. Section 4 analyses the wireless coverage parameters for mobile networks and Sect. 5 shows edge to edge service migration. Section 6 looks at the experimental test-bed and results in detail. Section 7 concludes the paper.

2   Literature Review

In order to analyse the effects of EC on reducing web response time authors in [6] derived a formula that reduces the response time of web pages by delivering objects from edge nodes. They investigated the effect of edge computing in different web categories such as sports and news. They were able to achieve this with their numerical evaluations using the data obtained by browsing about 1,000 web pages from 12 locations in the world.

Furthermore, authors of [5] proposed a model for system latency of two distributed processing scenarios by analysing the system latency of EC for multimedia data processing in the pipeline and parallel processing scenarios. They highlighted that both models can follow the actual characteristics of system latency. With regard to delay constrained offloading for MEC in cloud-enabled vehicular networks, the authors in [25] proposed a vehicular offloading framework in a cloud-based MEC environment. They were able to investigate the computation offloading mechanism. The latency and the resource limitations of MEC servers were taken into consideration which enabled the proposal of a computation, resource allocation and a contract-based offloading scheme. The scheme intends to exploit the utility of the MEC service provider to satisfy the offloading requirements of the task.

Given the significance of increased research in combining networking with MEC to support the development of 5G, the authors in [19] investigated the conceivable outcomes of engaging coordinated fiber-wireless (Fi-Wi) to get networks to offer MEC abilities. More predominantly, planned deployments of MEC over Fi-Wi networks for typical Radio Access Network(RAN) advancements were explored, representing both network architecture and enhanced resource management. Moreover, authors of [24] showed the architectural description of a MEC platform along with the key functionalities. They agreed that the RAN is enhanced by the computation and storage capacity provided using MEC. The primary benefit of MEC is to allow significant latency reduction to applications and services as well as reduced bandwidth consumption. The enhancement of RAN with the MECs capability can rely on its edge server cloud resources to provide the context-aware services to nearby mobile users in addition to conducting the packet forwarding.

For performance evaluation of edge cloud computing systems for big data applications, acceptable performance was revealed in [2] using Hadoop to build a visualisation machine for small clouds. In [10,20,21], the intended functioning of the projected system has been presented in an attempt to determine if the migration of a service is required. The proposed model allows services to migrate from one cloud to another. Kikuchi et al. [7] proposed a MEC-based VM migration scheme whereby a VM migration is conducted to reduce congestion at the edge of the network. They addressed two QoS problems which were the congestion in a wireless access network and congestion in computing resources on an edge with the use of TCP throughput.

Kim et al. [8] did a study on service instance allocation algorithms to maintain the QoS for mobile user with the help of a service migration tool. They were able to show simulations and compared their result to a heuristic algorithm and reference algorithms. This led to the understanding that their proposed algorithm performed better in a larger user population imbalance.

Recently, the ability of using low cost devices that have virtualization services was regarded as a better alternative to support computational requirements at the edge of a network. Lertsinsrubtavee et al. [9] introduced PiCasso, which is a lightweight service orchestration at the edge of the network. They further analysed and discussed their benchmarking results which enabled them to identify important parameters PiCasso would need in order to be taken into considerations for use in future network architecture.

A recent survey on architecture and computation offloading in MEC [11], explained that current research carried out regarding the MEC is basically how to guarantee service continuity in highly dynamic scenarios. They clearly state that this part is lacking in terms of research and is one of the stopping point to the use of the MEC concept in real world scenarios. Furthermore, they argued that recent validated research will not be acceptable due to their simplistic scenarios, simulations or analytical evaluations. Instead real tests and trials are further required in realistic scenarios.

With all the works mentioned above, the authors did not take into account the communication dynamics in highly mobile environments such as vehicular network i.e., handover in wireless network which is essential in order to provide a fully supported edge cloud computing environment and this is the focus of this paper.

3   Service Delivery for Mobile Clients

Current networks consist of three parts i.e., the core network, core end-point, and edge. The core network provides services to the users and has high computation, memory, and storage capacity. The core end-points are the end devices such as routers which enables communication and connectivity to other clouds and the edge network. Edge network consist of edge servers, access point, base station, etc., and has relatively low computation, memory, and storage capacity compared to the core network.

Providing services to the highly mobile system such as a vehicular network with high QoS is a key challenge in the future networks as the MN will be switching to different networks due to mobility. In order to address this challenge several works have proposed service migration as a solution. Service migration involves continuous migration of services closer to users as they move around resulting in reduced latency and better QoE [24]. For example, let us consider a scenario as shown in Fig. 1, where the cloud server is in the core network, routers are Core Endpoints, wireless access points are at the edge network and the MN as the client. There are four possible cases as described below:

- **Case 1:** A mobile user is travelling in a car and the user experiences a service offered by the core network i.e. the cloud that offers the service and the client receives it.
- **Case 2:** The service is running from the Core Endpoint, therefore, the delay between the Core Endpoint and the client should be lower than the case 1.
- **Case 3:** Services are running at the edge i.e., Edge server, Access point, etc. Therefore, the delay should be lower than the previous cases.
- **Case 4:** Here, the service are running within the client. This will be useful when the users have enough computing, memory and storage resources.

In this paper, we study the impact of service migration between the edge access points in a vehicular network which is called the Road-side Unit (RSU) in order to support better QoS for highly mobile nodes. There are several factors or functional requirements that have to be considered in migration of a service as explained below [20]:

- **Requirements 1:** A service needs to be recognisable by a unique ID and guaranteed to a set of parameters that can interoperate with the platform providers. The minimum required parameters must include CPU time, memory and storage, security protocols, network bandwidth and latency, and dependencies on other services.

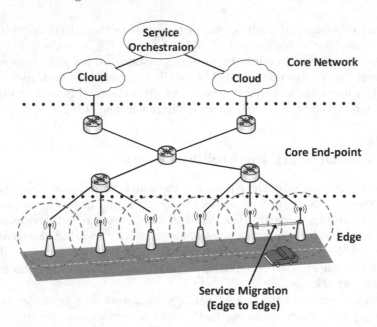

Fig. 1. Service migration scenario

- **Requirements 2:** The service should allow personalisation in terms of performance by the user, this would enable a user to make upgrades in terms of extra features or services. These parameters may include: maximum latency, a fixed allocated bandwidth to the user, security level, amount of storage, as well as taking into account the mobility of the user.
- **Requirements 3:** Platform providers (Clouds) can accept or reject services based on their set of requirements. They are required to bill service providers for processing, network and storage usage for any services and additional components running on their Cloud infrastructure. Furthermore, Cloud provider have the ability to decide which technology should be used for service migrations as long as it meets the service's minimum requirements.
- **Requirements 4:** To provide maximum benefits to their users, services have to be aware of their QoS level on a per-client basis. A server should stay alert in order to be aware of the client's network provider and current location. Such data can be gathered directly by the service and its processes, the client's device or a transport protocol that can report such information. This information will help to determine when and where to migrate.
- **Requirements 5:** If a service is requesting migration, it must pass information about the client's network provider to the platform provider to allow the finding of the best alternative Cloud to host the service. If possible a Cloud that is directly peering or local to the client's network.
- **Requirements 6:** Any Cloud offering resources for incoming services should report nominal values of network latency and bandwidth to the user's network. This helps to ensure that an incoming service will not only have

sufficient Cloud resources to run but also satisfactory network performance to deliver its content at the QoS demanded by the client.

– **Requirements 7:** The Serviced clients should have the ability to select the best possible network for handover via a querying mechanism which will confirm that the desired QoS level is deliverable through the new network. Therefore, clients will not rely on reported nominal values to determine the best network for service. If a handover to a network with less QoS is imminent, the service should migrate to an appropriate location (if it exists) to better the QoS.

Based on several requirements mentioned above the service migration time (ST) i.e, the time taken to migrate a service will be developed. In a highly mobile environment, ST is not the only parameter that can be used to decide whether a service can be migrated or not. In addition to the ST, the mobility aspects of the user has to be considered i.e, the time MN is expected to spend in the network coverage. If ST is greater than communication time (within the coverage region) then, by the time the service is migrated, the MN will be out of the coverage region, therefore, the service will not be successful. For example, Let us assume it takes 20 s to migrate a service from one RSU to another, when a MN is moving to the next coverage region and spends more than 20 s then service can be migrated and the service can be received from the RSU. But if the MN is spending less than 20 s in the new network then communication would be void because MN will be out of the coverage region. The following section will describe in detail the communication and mobility aspects in a highly mobile environments.

4   Wireless Coverage Parameters for Mobile Networks

In this section, we introduce a set of network coverage parameters that will be used in the following sections to demonstrate the service migration in highly mobile environment. The network coverage area is a region with an irregular shape where signals from a given Point of Attachment (PoA) i.e., Access Point or Base Station can be detected by a MN. The signals from the PoA are unreliable at the boundary and beyond the coverage area as the signals from the PoA cannot be detected. For seamless communication, handover should be finished before the coverage boundary is reached.

Therefore, a circle known as the handover radius (R_H) and exit radius (R_E) was defined in [13] to ensure smooth handover. The work states that the handover must begin at the exit radius and should be completed before reaching the handover radius boundary as shown in Fig. 2.

The exit radius will therefore be dependent on the velocity, ν, of the MN. If we represent the time taken to execute a handover by T_{EH}, then:

$$T_{EH} \leq \frac{(R_H - R_E)}{\nu} \tag{1}$$

Hence, exit radius can be given as shown in Eq. (2)

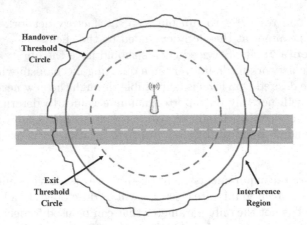

Fig. 2. Network coverage

$$R_E \leq R_H - (\nu * T_{EH}) \tag{2}$$

So, the faster a MN moves, the smaller the R_E at which handover must begin. Given that we know the time taken to execute a handover, the velocity of the MN and handover radius, then we can calculate the exit radius which is dependent on the handover radius. A good estimation of the handover radius is required for the proposed approach which is dependent on the propagation models being used. The time taken to effect a handover was shown to be dependent on various factors such as Detection Time (t_{det}), Configuration Time (t_{con}), Registration Time (t_{reg}) and Adaptation Time (t_{adp}) as discussed in [13].

Our previous work on proactive handover in [14] showed that the above-mentioned coverage parameters can be segmented into communication ranges and presented an in-depth analysis of such segmentation and their importance in-order to achieve a seamless handover as shown in Fig. 3. This segmentation can be put into effective use for achieving proactive handover, resource allocation, and service migration for a highly mobile environment.

Time before handover (Υ) is the time after which the handover process should start and Time to handover ($\hbar$) is the time before which the handover to next coverage range has to be completed. Network Dwell Time ($\aleph$) is the time MN will spend in the coverage i.e., the Network Dwell Distance (NDD) of new network.

Resource Hold Time ($\mathbb{N}$) is the resource usage time or when actual exchange of data is taking place. $\hbar$ and $\mathbb{N}$ are the two key parameters that has to be considered for service migration in highly mobile networks.

5   Edge to Edge Service Migration

Let's suppose the MN is travelling at a velocity, ν from one RSU's coverage region to the next one: with an estimate of the Υ, $\hbar$ and $\mathbb{N}$, it is possible to

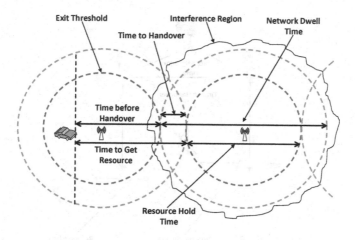

Fig. 3. Communication range segmentation

decide whether a service should be migrated with the knowledge of ST. Hence, ST should be less than the sum of $\hbar$ and $\mathbb{N}$ in order to have a seamless service. If the ST is greater than the sum of $\hbar$ and $\mathbb{N}$ then the MN will be out of coverage of the next RSU due to mobility by the time the service is migrated. Therefore, in order to get effective service

$$(\hbar + \mathbb{N}) > ST \tag{3}$$

Hence, for a seamless service to the MN the ratio of the communication times due to mobility and the service migration time has to be always greater than 1 as shown in the equation below. Here, $\hbar$ is usually very small as it is the time taken to handover.

$$\frac{(\hbar + \mathbb{N})}{ST} > 1 \tag{4}$$

The above equation denotes a reactive approach i.e., the service migration will only start after the MN reaches the next RSU's coverage. Therefore, when the MN reaches the next coverage range where $\Upsilon = 0$, i.e, during handover, the serivce will be migrated to the next RSU. In summary, communication and service handover takes place at the same time, this is called a reactive communication and service handover. The reactive migration approach might disrupt the service due to mobility for services with higher migration time. Hence, we need a proactive service migration to be adopted for better QoS and QoE.

In the proposed proactive approach the service migration will begin before the Υ i.e., before the communication handover as shown in Fig. 4. The point where the service is starting to migrate is called as proactive service migration time (X). When the service begins to migrate at point X before the communication handover, so the amount of time left is ST-X. This means that, X should be less

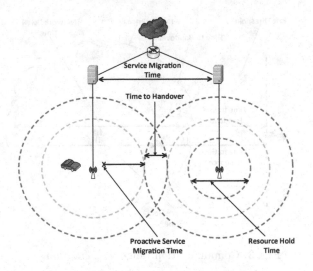

Fig. 4. Service migration segmentation

than or equal to ST, which will ensure that the service is not migrated far ahead before the MN reaches the coverage. Therefore,

$$(\hbar + \mathbb{N}) > (ST - X) \tag{5}$$

As explained earlier for a seamless service to the MN the ratio of the communication times due to mobility and the service migration time has to always be greater than 1 as shown below:

$$\frac{(\hbar + \mathbb{N})}{(ST - X)} > 1 \tag{6}$$

6   Experimental Framework

In order to explore Eq. 6, the values of the parameters $\hbar$ and $\mathbb{N}$ were obtained using a VANET test-bed. In addition, the Service Time (ST) was obtained for different applications and services which include No application, Game server, RAM Simulation, Video Streaming, and Face Detection. These applications were fully explored in a previous paper and accurate values of ST were obtained and used later in the paper to calculate service migration ratio as shown in Eq. 6.

6.1   Experimental Test-Bed and Results

This section provides the details of the real experimental VANET test-bed. The Connected Vehicle Test-bed, was built by Middlesex University and the Department of Transport (DfT) using ETSI Intelligent Transport System (ITS) G5 (VANET) technology [15]. The test-beds were built on the Hendon Campus in

London and alongside the surrounding roads. The test-bed uses seven RSUs and also extends to the A41 (Watford Way) behind the campus. Four RSUs, which were deployed on the MDX buildings, were backhauled directly to the university's gigabit ethernet network and the three RSUs deployed along the A41 were backhauled using LTE with a secure VPN tunnel service provided by Mobius Network as shown in Fig. 5. They are now fully operational and trials have been held to fully understand the technology and concerns around its wide-scale deployment as well as communication dynamics needed to attain seamless communication for this environment.

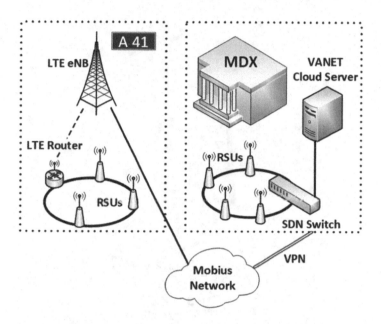

Fig. 5. MDX VANET testbed network diagram

The coverage map of this testbed is as shown in Fig. 6. The NDD for each RSU was measured from the coverage map and with the NDD, the $\aleph$ can be calculated if the velocity of the vehicle is known. Table 1 shows the $\aleph$ and $\mathbb{N}$ for two different velocities i.e., 30 Mph and 50 Mph for all the RSUs. We know from [13] that the handover execution time i.e., $\hbar$ is 4s and therefore, the $\mathbb{N}$ is:

$$\mathbb{N} = \aleph - \hbar \tag{7}$$

With the knowledge of the mobility, $\mathbb{N}$, $\hbar$, and in addition, if the ST can be estimated, then we can efficiently decide when and where to migrate a service. The following subsection will present the result of our approach.

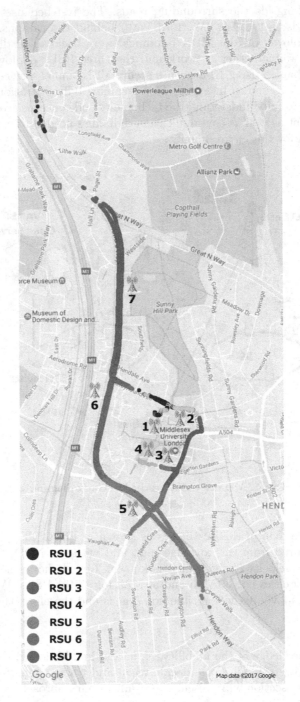

Fig. 6. Full coverage and overlapping map for A41, Watford Way, Hendon, London

Table 1. Communication coverage segmentation distance and time ($\hbar = 4\,s$).

RSU No.	NDD	30 Mph		50 Mph	
		$\aleph$	N	$\aleph$	N
RSU 1	300 m	22.37 s	18.37	13.42 s	9.42 s
RSU 2	456 m	34.00 s	30.00 s	20.40 s	16.40 s
RSU 3	517 m	38.55 s	34.55 s	23.13 s	19.13 s
RSU 4	248 m	18.49 s	14.49 s	11.09 s	7.09 s
RSU 5	974 m	72.63 s	68.63 s	43.57 s	39.57 s
RSU 6	1390 m	103.64 s	99.64 s	62.19 s	58.19 s
RSU 7	1140 m	85.00 s	81.00 s	51.00 s	47.00 s

6.2 Live Service Migration Use Case Scenario Results

Moving a service across the edge nodes is an essential factor with regards to ensuring that users have good performance with proximity especially in a highly mobile network like vehicular networks. This section investigates the impact of live service migration within a VANET environment by making use of the results collected from the real experimental VANET test-bed as well as the results for ST presented in [12] for different services. We have considered two RSUs; RSU 2 located at Williams building and RSU 3 located at Hatchcroft building. The scenario considered was a MN travelling at two different velocities i.e., 30 Mph and 50 Mph which is being handing over from RSU 3 to RSU 2. The NDD of these RSUs from the MDX VANET test-bed has been used in this paper to demonstrate the effectiveness of our service migration model.

The authors in [12] detail a layered framework for migrating active service applications which are condensed in virtual machines (VMs) and containers. Containers are a developing technology and they consume less storage space compared to VMs, therefore, will be appropriate for service migration. Under the given framework, the migration performance in terms of ST for both VM and containers were examined in a controlled test-bed environment. They have considered five different applications for migration; No Application, Game Server, RAM Simulation, Video Streaming and Face Detection. The results on the performance of two i.e., 2 layer and 3 layer approaches for different applications with container technology as shown in Table 2 have been used in this work for the evaluation of our model.

Given the measurement results for service migration as listed in Table 2, we consider two use-cases for two different velocities i.e., 30 Mph and 50 Mph:

– Reactive Approach where the service migration starts once the MN reaches the next RSU's coverage region.
– Proactive Approach where the service migration starts before the MN reaches the next RSU's coverage region at point X called the proactive service migration time.

Table 2. Migration results for two-layer and three layer configurations [12]

Services	ST/data transferred	
	2 layer	3 layer
No Application	6.5 s/1.4 MB	11.0 s/1.9 MB
Game Server	7.3 s/2.2 MB	10.9 s/2.7 MB
RAM Simulation	20.2 s/97.1 MB	27.2 s/97.6 MB
Video Streaming	27.5 s/180.2 MB	37.3 s/184.6 MB
Face Detection	52.0 s/363.1 MB	70.1 s/365.0 MB

The graphs presented in Figs. 7 and 8 show the ratio for reactive and proactive service migration derived from Eqs. 4 and 6 respectively for different application services presented in Table 2. For a service to be successfully migrated the ratio has to be above 1, which is the threshold.

In case 1, we can observe that the service migration in a mobile environment is successful for both No application, and Game server with 2 layer and 3 layer approach for both 30 Mph and 50 Mph as shown in Fig. 7. This is due to the fact that the size of the service is small compared to others. RAM Simulation service cannot be successfully migrated for 3 layer approach at 50 Mph, this is due to the high speed and rest of the cases for RAM Simulation service can be successfully migrated. The other two services i.e, Video streaming and Face detection cannot be migrated in a reactive service migration.

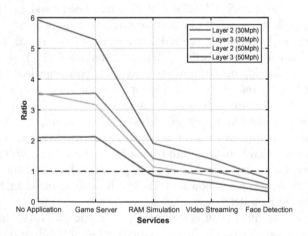

Fig. 7. Service migration for reactive handover

In case 2, Fig. 8 shows the results of proactive approach i.e, service is migrated at the proactive service migration time, X. This is not a constant value and it changes according to the type of the service. We consider the values of X (in seconds) for No Application and Game server as 5 s, RAM simulation and video streaming to be 15 s and then finally face detection as 45 s. The results show that the No Application, Game server, and RAM Simulation are successfully migrated for all cases. Video streaming, and Face detection are almost nearing the threshold 1 for 3 layer approach at 50 Mph and all other cases can be successfully migrated. This shows the need for a proactive service migration approach in a highly mobile edge environment. In addition, proactive service migration time, X has to be explored in the future to develop efficient algorithms for such service migration. Here, the ST was measured in a controlled environment and therefore, estimating the ST in real-time is necessary.

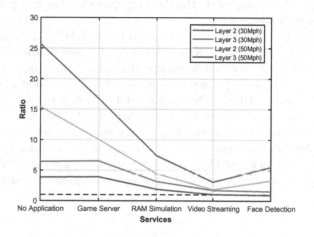

Fig. 8. Service migration for proactive handover

6.3 Transport Protocol Performance Evaluation over VANET

To be able to estimate the ST in real time, the underlying transport protocol plays a significant role. In this context, this section compares the performance of two transport protocols: Simple Lightweight Transport Protocol (SLTP) and Transmission Control Protocol (TCP). The details on SLTP functionality and its internal structure can be found in [18]. The aim is to demonstrate the effectiveness of SLTP as a low latency protocol which works by measuring the service time based on the available bandwidth. Two sets of experiments are conducted

- RSU to VANET server link performance
- RSU to RSU link performance.

Our first set of results will look at SLTP running at the VANET server and the RSU. Packets of different sizes were sent and the time taken to receive them back at the sender was measured. This gives us a direct measurement of protocol performance. We performed our benchmarks by using the following hardware specifications as shown in Table 3 for the VANET server and the RSU. It can be

Table 3. Hardware specifications

Specifications	VANET server	RSU
Processor	Intel (R) Xeon (R) CPU E5-2683 v4	MIPS 24Kc V7.4 (1 core)
RAM	32 GB	64 MB SDRAM (512 Mbits)
Storage	500 GB	16 MB Flash
Network	1 Gigabit Ethernet	1 Gigabit Ethernet
OS Type	Debian 3.16.43 (64 Bit)	Debian 2.6.32.27 (32 Bit)

clearly seen that the resources on the RSU are quite limited compared with the VANET server or a modern PC.

Since SLTP runs over User Datagram Protocol (UDP), the size of a single SLTP packet can be up to (64 KBs - 8 bytes, the size of the UDP header). However, for testing we wanted to ensure that SLTP packets could fit into a whole number of Ethernet packets which can carry a payload of 1500 bytes. This means that each SLTP packet contained 1452 bytes of user data which is comparable to the packet utilization of standard TCP. Though SLTP supports a window size of 1 MB, it was decided to use a window size of 144 KBs to ensure that received buffers were not overrun. The result, shown in Fig. 9, indicates that in this arrangement, less CPU cycles as well as memory are available on the RSU and hence, the performance of SLTP is not much greater than the standard TCP.

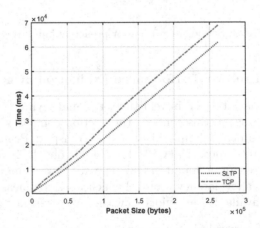

Fig. 9. RSU to VANET server - network time: SLTP vs TCP

Finally, the results for RSU to RSU are given in Fig. 10. These results show that with two RSUs there is very limited resources at user level and hence, TCP in the kernel will outperform SLTP. Overall, these graphs indicate that to get good performance in user space requires an abundance of CPU, memory and network resources which is an important factor for service migration at the edge.

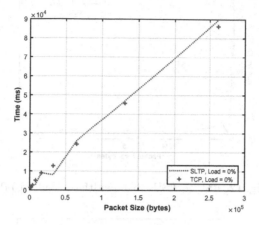

Fig. 10. RSU to RSU - network time on load = 0%: SLTP vs TCP

6.4   RSU to RSU Link Performance Under Different Load Conditions

Since, SLTP runs in user space, it is important to understand how its performance is affected by different load characteristics of the system. In order to explore this, a flexible hog program was used to remove idle CPU cycles at the user level from the system. Hence, we were able to obtain readings with the system being under various loads, including 25%, 50%, 75% and 100%.

Figure 11 shows the time taken to transfer packets of different buffer sizes under different loads and it clearly shows that as the load increases SLTP underperforms TCP as less cycles are available in user space.

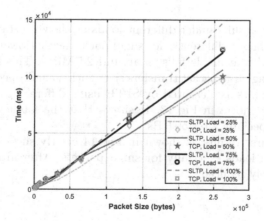

Fig. 11. RSU to RSU - network time on load = 25% to 100%: SLTP vs TCP

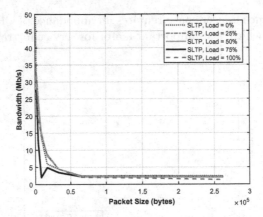

Fig. 12. RSU to RSU - bandwidth on load: SLTP

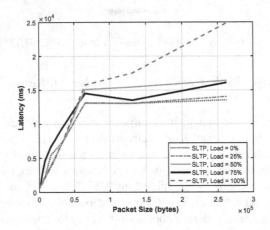

Fig. 13. RSU to RSU - latency on load: SLTP

The bandwidth results under different loads as shown in Fig. 12 reveal that there are only significant differences for small packet sizes. However, after around 2 KBs the bandwidth available falls to around 2.5 MB/s. This is important for applications needing large packet transfers sizes such as multimedia applications.

The latency results as measured by SLTP using different packet sizes under different loads are shown in Fig. 13. It shows that the latency increases with increasing load especially after 50 KBs.

Finally, the burst results as shown in Fig. 14 clearly show that the system is affected by high loads especially for small packets. After around 10 KBs the burst size is severely reduced.

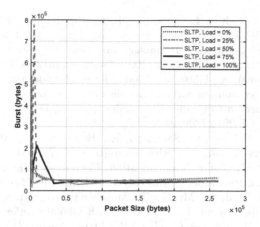

Fig. 14. RSU to RSU - burst on load: SLTP

7 Conclusion

The dynamics of the wireless environment makes the provisioning of guaranteed QoS a significant challenge especially within highly mobile environments like VANET. In this context, intelligent MEC is seen as part of the solution. This paper studies the impact of integrating MEC within VANET in terms of mobility, handover and service migration between edge access points for different applications. Additionally, a new service migration threshold model is proposed. The results collected from a real experimental vehicular network test-bed were used to better understand the impact of live service migration within a VANET environment in the context of reactive versus proactive service migration scenarios. The results show that a proactive service migration is more efficient within a MEC-VANET environment. Additionally, we investigated the performance of the underlying transport protocol and demonstrated its impact in the context of live service migration for highly mobile environments.

References

1. Barbarossa, S., Sardellitti, S., Lorenzo, P.D.: Communicating while computing: distributed mobile cloud computing over 5G heterogeneous networks. IEEE Signal Process. Mag. **31**(6), 45–55 (2014). https://doi.org/10.1109/MSP.2014.2334709
2. Femminella, M., Pergolesi, M., Reali, G.: Performance evaluation of edge cloud computing system for big data applications. In: 2016 5th IEEE International Conference on Cloud Networking (Cloudnet), pp. 170–175, October 2016. https://doi.org/10.1109/CloudNet.2016.56
3. Dinh, H.T., Lee, C., Niyato, D., Wang, P.: A survey of mobile cloud computing: architecture, applications, and approaches. Wirel. Commun. Mob. Comput. **13**, 1587–1611 (2013)

4. Hussain, R., Son, J., Eun, H., Kim, S., Oh, H.: Rethinking vehicular communications: Merging VANET with cloud computing. In: 4th IEEE International Conference on Cloud Computing Technology and Science Proceedings, pp. 606–609, December 2012. https://doi.org/10.1109/CloudCom.2012.6427481

5. Imagane, K., Kanai, K., Katto, J., Tsuda, T.: Evaluation and analysis of system latency of edge computing for multimedia data processing. In: 2016 IEEE 5th Global Conference on Consumer Electronics, pp. 1–2, October 2016. https://doi.org/10.1109/GCCE.2016.7800393

6. Kamiyama, N., Nakano, Y., Shiomoto, K., Hasegawa, G., Murata, M., Miyahara, H.: Analyzing effect of edge computing on reduction of web response time. In: 2016 IEEE Global Communications Conference (GLOBECOM), pp. 1–6, December 2016. https://doi.org/10.1109/GLOCOM.2016.7841607

7. Kikuchi, J., Wu, C., Ji, Y., Murase, T.: Mobile edge computing based VM migration for QoS improvement. In: 2017 IEEE 6th Global Conference on Consumer Electronics (GCCE), pp. 1–5, October 2017. https://doi.org/10.1109/GCCE.2017.8229344

8. Kim, S.Y., de Foy, X., Reznik, A.: Practical service allocation in mobile edge computing systems. In: 2017 27th International Telecommunication Networks and Applications Conference (ITNAC), pp. 1–6, November 2017. https://doi.org/10.1109/ATNAC.2017.8215372

9. Lertsinsrubtavee, A., Ali, A., Molina-Jimenez, C., Sathiaseelan, A., Crowcroft, J.: PiCasso: a lightweight edge computing platform. In: 2017 IEEE 6th International Conference on Cloud Networking (CloudNet), pp. 1–7, September 2017. https://doi.org/10.1109/CloudNet.2017.8071529

10. Li, H., Shou, G., Hu, Y., Guo, Z.: Mobile edge computing: progress and challenges. In: 2016 4th IEEE International Conference on Mobile Cloud Computing, Services, and Engineering (MobileCloud), pp. 83–84, March 2016. https://doi.org/10.1109/MobileCloud.2016.16

11. Mach, P., Becvar, Z.: Mobile edge computing: a survey on architecture and computation offloading. IEEE Commun. Surv. Tutor. 19(3), 1628–1656 (2017). https://doi.org/10.1109/COMST.2017.2682318

12. Machen, A., Wang, S., Leung, K.K., Ko, B.J., Salonidis, T.: Live service migration in mobile edge clouds. IEEE Wirel. Commun. 25(1), 140–147 (2018). https://doi.org/10.1109/MWC.2017.1700011

13. Mapp, G., et al.: Exploiting location and contextual information to develop a comprehensive framework for proactive handover in heterogeneous environments. J. Comput. Netw. Commun. 2012, 1–17, Article ID 748163 (2012). https://doi.org/10.1155/2012/748163

14. Mapp, G., Gosh, A., Paranthaman, V.V., Iniovosa, V.O., Loo, J., Vinel, A.: Exploring seamless connectivity and proactive handover techniques in VANET systems. In: Alam, M., Ferreira, J., Fonseca, J. (eds.) Intelligent Transportation Systems. SSDC, vol. 52, pp. 195–220. Springer, Cham (2016). https://doi.org/10.1007/978-3-319-28183-4_9

15. Paranthaman, V.V., et al.: Building a prototype VANET testbed to explore communication dynamics in highly mobile environments. In: Guo, S., Wei, G., Xiang, Y., Lin, X., Lorenz, P. (eds.) TridentCom 2016. LNICST, vol. 177, pp. 81–90. Springer, Cham (2017). https://doi.org/10.1007/978-3-319-49580-4_8

16. Khan, A.U.R., Othman, M., Madani, S.A., Khan, S.U.: A survey of mobile cloud computing application models. IEEE Commun. Surv. Tutor. 16(1), 393–413 (2014). https://doi.org/10.1109/SURV.2013.062613.00160

17. Ren, J., Guo, H., Xu, C., Zhang, Y.: Serving at the edge: a scalable IoT architecture based on transparent computing. IEEE Netw. **31**(5), 96–105 (2017). https://doi.org/10.1109/MNET.2017.1700030

18. Riley, L., Mapp, G: yRFC3: the specification of SP-Lite. http://www.mdx.ac.uk/our-research/research-groups/y-comm-global-research-group/y-comm-research

19. Rimal, B.P., Van, D.P., Maier, M.: Mobile edge computing empowered fiber-wireless access networks in the 5G era. IEEE Commun. Mag. **55**(2), 192–200 (2017). https://doi.org/10.1109/MCOM.2017.1600156CM

20. Sardis, F.: Exploring traffic and QoS management mechanisms to support mobile cloud computing using service localisation in heterogeneous environments. Ph.D. thesis (2014)

21. Sardis, F., Mapp, G., Loo, J., Aiash, M., Vinel, A.: On the investigation of cloud-based mobile media environments with service-populating and QoS-aware mechanisms. IEEE Trans. Multimed. **15**(4), 769–777 (2013). https://doi.org/10.1109/TMM.2013.2240286

22. Sun, X., Ansari, N.: EdgeIoT: mobile edge computing for the Internet of Things. IEEE Commun. Mag. **54**(12), 22–29 (2016). https://doi.org/10.1109/MCOM.2016.1600492CM

23. Tran, T.X., Hajisami, A., Pandey, P., Pompili, D.: Collaborative mobile edge computing in 5G networks: new paradigms, scenarios, and challenges. IEEE Commun. Mag. **55**(4), 54–61 (2017). https://doi.org/10.1109/MCOM.2017.1600863

24. Yu, Y.: Mobile edge computing towards 5G: vision, recent progress, and open challenges. China Commun. **13**(Suppl. 2), 89–99 (2016). https://doi.org/10.1109/CC.2016.7833463

25. Zhang, K., Mao, Y., Leng, S., Vinel, A., Zhang, Y.: Delay constrained offloading for mobile edge computing in cloud-enabled vehicular networks. In: 2016 8th International Workshop on Resilient Networks Design and Modeling (RNDM), pp. 288–294, September 2016. https://doi.org/10.1109/RNDM.2016.7608300

A Balanced Cloudlet Management Method for Wireless Metropolitan Area Networks

Xiaolong Xu[1,2,3(✉)], Yuhao Chen[1,2], Lianyong Qi[4], Jing He[1,2],
and Xuyun Zhang[5]

[1] School of Computer and Software,
Nanjing University of Information Science and Technology, Nanjing, China
njuxlxu@gmail.com
[2] Jiangsu Engineering Centre of Network Monitoring,
Nanjing University of Information Science and Technology, Nanjing, China
[3] State Key Laboratory for Novel Software Technology,
Nanjing University, Nanjing, China
[4] School of Information Science and Engineering, Qufu Normal University,
Jining, China
[5] Department of Electrical and Computer Engineering, University of Auckland,
Auckland, New Zealand

Abstract. With the rapid development of wireless communication technology, cloudlet-based wireless metropolitan area network, which provides people with more convenient network services, has become an effiective paradigm to meet the growing demand for requirements of wireless cloud computing. Currently, the energy consumption of cloudlets can be reduced by migrating tasks, but how to jointly optimize the time consumption and energy consumption in the process of migrations is still a significant problem. In this paper, a balanced cloudlet management method, named BCM, is proposed to address the above challenge. Technically, the Simple Additive Weighting (SAW) and Multiple Criteria Decision Making (MCDM) techniques are applied to optimize virtual machine scheduling strategy. Finally, simulation results demonstrate the effectiveness of our proposed method.

Keywords: Cloudlet · WMAN · VM migration ·
Energy consumption · Time consumption

1 Introduction

In recent years, to meet the growing demand for the requirements of wireless cloud computing, wireless metropolitan area network (WMAN) has emerged as a public network in the society, providing people with more convenient network services [1]. Computing tasks of mobile devices are migrated from mobile devices to remote data centers through access points in WMAN. With the increasing

© ICST Institute for Computer Sciences, Social Informatics and Telecommunications Engineering 2019
Published by Springer Nature Switzerland AG 2019. All Rights Reserved
H. Gao et al. (Eds.): TridentCom 2018, LNICST 270, pp. 62–75, 2019.
https://doi.org/10.1007/978-3-030-12971-2_4

popularity of mobile devices and the maturing of wireless communication technology, WMAN achieves great development with its excellent features in coverage, transmission speed and comprehensive cost [2].

Nowadays, the wide spread of smart phones and their powerful functions have made them an important part of many people's life over the world [3]. A variety of mobile applications have been developed to bring people more convenience and enrich their lives. However, the content-rich and powerful applications increase the resource cost of mobile devices. Due to many restrictions, such as large quantities of energy consumption and application running time, mobile devices are often difficult to meet the resource requirements of the applications [4].

As a new type of business computing mode, cloud computing can provide users with high reliability, dynamic and scalable virtual computing resources in a on-demand way. Users can enter the configurable computing resources shared pool and get access to resources quickly [5].When faced with complex mobile applications which require a large amount of computation source, mobile devices often choose to migrate these tasks to a cloud resource center for better performance and less energy consumption [6]. In a complex wireless network environment, for the traditional mobile cloud computing architecture, a cloud is generally located far away from mobile users, which inevitably leads to the communication delay between mobile devices and the cloud [7]. In service framework of WMAN, cloudlets as edge devices are widely used to reduce end-to-end communication delay [8,9].

Cloudlets are deployed closed to users to provide rich data storage and computing resources [10]. Generally, a large number of cloudlets and access points are deployed in WMAN environment. Users can easily access to cloudlets through APs in WMAN for fast and efficient computation [8]. With the constant promotion and popularity of cloud computing technology, the number of cloudlet consumers is increasing rapidly. When there are only few tasks executing on a cloudlet, the running cloudlet will waste large quantities of energy. Compared with it, it will be more energy-saving to migrate the tasks to other cloudlets and close the running cloudlet. Generally, users migrate computing tasks to a cloudlet in the form of virtual machine (VM) [11]. Though the number of running cloudlets decreases sharply after several migrations, excessive time consumption and energy consumption during migrations are both big problems which are often ignored.

In the view of this challenge, a VM scheduling method for balancing energy consumption and time consumption in wireless metropolitan area network is proposed in this paper. The main contributions of this paper can be summarized in three folds. Firstly, we formulate a problem for reducing the two objectives, time consumption and energy consumption. Secondly, a balanced cloudlet management method, named BCM, is proposed to achieve the goal. In this method, the Simple Additive Weighting (SAW) and Multiple Criteria Decision Making (MCDM) techniques are applied to optimize scheduling strategy. Finally, comprehensive experiments are conducted to verify the effectiveness of our proposed method.

The rest of this paper is organized as follows. Section 2 formulates a problem for reducing energy consumption and time consumption in cloudlet environment. In section 3, a balanced cloudlet management method named BCM is proposed. Then several experiments are conducted, and the results are presented in Sect. 4. Finally, Sect. 5 analyzes the related work and Sect. 6 states the conclusion and future work.

2   Problem Formulation

In this section, We formulate a problem for reducing energy consumption and time consumption in WMAN. Key terms used in the formulation are listed in Table 1.

Table 1. Key terms and descriptions

Term	Description
C	The set of running cloudlets, $C = \{c_1, c_2, \ldots, c_N\}$
W	The set of access point(AP), $W = \{w_1, w_2, \ldots, w_Q\}$
V	The set of running VM, $V = \{v_1, v_2, \ldots, v_M\}$
$E_{Active}(t)$	The energy consumption of the running VMs
$t_{MP}^n(t)$	The running time of the n-th cloudlet
$E_{Idle}(t)$	The energy consumed by idle VMs
$E_{Base}(t)$	The basic energy consumption of cloudlets
$T_{edge}^n(t)$	The time consumed by transmission between cloudlets and APs
$T_{mid}^n(t)$	The time consumed by migration from a AP_{sour} to the AP_{desc}
$P_q(t)$	The energy consumption rate of the q-th AP W_q
$E_{AP}(t)$	The energy consumption of APs
$E_{Oper}(t)$	The energy consumption of opening/closing operation
$E_{All}(t)$	All the energy consumption
$T_{All}(t)$	All the time consumption

2.1   Basic Concepts

We assume that there are N cloudlets and Q access points in WMAN, denoted as $C = \{c_1, c_2, \ldots, c_N\}$ and $W = \{w_1, w_2, \ldots, w_Q\}$, respectively. Consider a scenario, only one physical machine(PM) is deployed in each cloudlet. Besides, we assume that there are M VMs running in cloudlets, denoted as $V = \{v_1, v_2, \ldots, v_M\}$.

Figure 1. shows an example of task migration in cloudlet-based WMAN. There are a certain amount of APs between two cloudlets. The AP next to the source cloudlet and the AP next to the destination cloudlet are named as AP_{sour} and AP_{desc}, respectively. The AP between a AP_{sour} and a AP_{desc} is named as AP_{mid}.

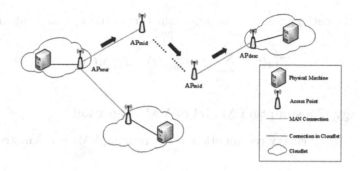

Fig. 1. An example of task migration in cloudlet-based WMAN

2.2 Time Consumption Model of VM Migration

To reduce the energy consumption, we shall migrate the VMs from hosted cloudlets to other cloudlets. However, the process of migration consumes a quantities of transmission time.

$I_m^n(t)$ is a binary variable to judge whether the v_m is placed on cloudlet c_n at time t, which is defined by

$$I_m^n(t) = \begin{cases} 1, & \text{if } v_m \text{ is placed on } c_n \\ 0, & \text{otherwise} \end{cases} \tag{1}$$

$M_m^{n,n'}t$ is a binary variable that indicates whether v_m is migrated from c_n to $c_{n'}$ at time t, which is defined as

$$M_m^{n,n'}(t) = \begin{cases} 1, & \text{if } v_m \text{ is migrated from } c_n \text{ to } c_{n'} \\ 0, & \text{otherwise.} \end{cases} \tag{2}$$

When the cloudlet c_n needs to be transferred between the cloudlet and the AP next to it, the time consumption is calculated by

$$T_{edge}^n(t) = \sum_{m=1}^{M} \sum_{n'=1}^{N} I_m^n(t) \cdot M_m^{n,n'}(t) \cdot \frac{d_m}{\rho}, \tag{3}$$

where d_m is the data size of the v_m, and ρ is the transmission efficiency between the cloudlet and the AP next to it.

Let $G_{n,n'}$ be the number of APs between the c_n and the $c_{n'}$, including a AP_{sour}, a AP_{desc} and several AP_{mid}s. The time consumed by migration from AP_{sour} to AP_{desc} is calculated by

$$T_{mid}^n(t) = \sum_{m=1}^{M} \sum_{n'=1}^{N} I_m^n(t) \cdot M_m^{n,n'}(t) \cdot \frac{d_m}{s} \cdot (G_{n,n'} - 1), \tag{4}$$

where s is the transmission efficiency between APs.

During the entire process of migration, the time consumption is calculated by

$$T_{All}(t) = \sum_{n=1}^{N} (2 \cdot T_{edge}^n(t) + T_{mid}^n(t)) \tag{5}$$

2.3   Energy Consumption Model of VM Migration

Based on [12], the energy consumption of the running VMs is calculated by

$$E_{Active}(t) = \sum_{m=1}^{M} \alpha_m \cdot \varphi_m(t) \tag{6}$$

where α_m is the energy consumption rate of the m-th VM, and $\varphi_m(t)$ indicates the execution time of the m-th VM v_m.

A cloudlet will continue running until all the tasks in this cloudlet have been excuted, thus the running time of the n-th cloudlet is calculated by

$$t_{MP}^n(t) = \max_{m=1}^{M} \{I_m^n(t) \cdot \varphi_m(t)\} \tag{7}$$

The energy consumed by idle VMs is calculated by

$$E_{Idle}(t) = \sum_{n=1}^{N} \sum_{m=1}^{M} \beta_m \cdot (t_{MP}^n - \varphi_m(t)) \tag{8}$$

where β_m is the energy consumption rate of the m-th VM v_m in idle mode.

The basic energy consumption of cloudlets is calculated by

$$E_{Base}(t) = \sum_{n=1}^{N} \gamma_n \cdot t_{MP}^n(t) \tag{9}$$

where γ_n is the basic energy consumption rate of the n-th cloudlet.

During the process of migration, APs shall consume energy due to the data transmission. Based on [13], the energy consumption rate of the q-th AP w_q is calculated by

$$P_q(t) = e_q + \eta_q p_q \cdot \sum_{p \in W} \frac{h_q}{r_{pq}} \tag{10}$$

where e_q, h_q, p_q, η_q and r_{pq} is the baseline power of the q-th AP w_q, the traffic demand of w_q, the signal transmission power of w_q, the signal transceiver power factor of w_q and the link rate between w_p and w_q, respectively.

The energy consumption of APs is calculated by

$$E_{AP}(t) = \sum_{q=1}^{Q} \int_{t}^{T_{All}(t)} P_q(t)dt \tag{11}$$

In this paper, the operation time of VM starting and closing is set to the same constant, which is denoted as g. The energy consumption of the starting/closing operation of the VM is calculated by

$$E_{Oper}(t) = \sum_{m=1}^{M} \sum_{n=1}^{N} \sum_{n'=1}^{N} 2g \cdot I_m^n(t) \cdot M_m^{n,n'}(t) \cdot \alpha_m \tag{12}$$

Based on the energy consumption model in [14], let $E_{All}(t)$ be all the energy consumed by both the APs and cloudlets, which is calculated by

$$E_{All}(t) = E_{Active}(t) + E_{Idle}(t) + E_{Base}(t) + E_{Oper}(t) + E_{AP}(t) \tag{13}$$

2.4 Problem Definition

From the above analysis, energy consumption model and time consumption model are built to quantify the two objectives. In this paper, how to evaluate the two influencing factors synthetically and minimize the consumption is our core issue. The problem is formulated by

$$min \; T_{All}(t), \; min \; E_{All}(t) \tag{14}$$

3 Balanced Cloudlet Management Method for WMAN

Based on the analysis in Sect. 2, a balanced cloudlet management method is proposed in this section. Our method mainly consists of two steps as in Fig. 2.

> **Step1:** VM migration strategy searching. Through a heuristic strategy, some possible VM migration strategies, which can determine where the VMs should be migrated to, are searched to form the migration composition set.
>
> **Step2:** Multi-objective optimization scheduling. The final VM scheduling strategy will be achieved through applying the SAW and MCDM techniques to compare the utility values of migration compositions which are obtained in Step 1.

Fig. 2. Specification of balanced cloudlet management method.

3.1 VM Migration Strategy Searching

The tasks hosted on a cloudlet usually have different numbers of VM requirements. Here, we assume that each cloudlet has only one PM. In Algorithm 1, we propose a method to find VM migration strategy.

Definition 1 (migration strategy ms_k): We define the scheme migrating a VM from hosted cloudlet to destination one as a migration strategy, which is denoted as $mc_k=(sp_k, ep_k, tc_k)$, where sp_k, ep_k and tc_k are the hosted cloudlet of the k-th VM, the destination cloudlet of the k-th VM and the time consumption of migration, respectively.

In this method, we only migrate VMs to the cloudlets with idle space, and the cloudlets which are running in full load will not be migration targets.

Definition 2 (migration composition mc_k): Through analysis, all the VMs of the same task should be migrated to the same cloudlet, thus we may get more than one migration strategy recording the source selection and allocation in the VM scheduling process at the same time. Generally, there are several tasks in one cloudlet. We name the set of migration strategies which migrate all the tasks of one cloudlet as a migration composition.

In Step 1, we sort the cloudlets in the decreasing order of idle VMs firstly, and migrate tasks from their hosted cloudlets to the destination cloudlets which have as little but enough idle space as possible. In the migration process, there may be more than one cloudlet to meet the requirements. To deal with these scene, we calculate the time consumption values caused by different choices with the formula (5) and select the strategy with minimum time consumption value. Then a temporal migration strategy is generated. If all the VMs in this cloudlet can be migrated away, a migration composition will be generated. Otherwise, the temporal strategies will be deleted. After acquiring a migration composition, the idle cloudlet will be turn off and all these cloudlets will be resorted. The next migration composition is generated by iteration. In other words, new migrations will be created on the basis of previous one until all the VMs can't be migrated.

Figure 3 shows an example of migration destination selection. c_1, c_2, c_3 and c_4 are four cloudlets running in a wireless metropolitan area network. Two tasks t_1 and t_2 need to be executed on c_1 which occupy two VMs and one VM respectively. Both of c_2 and c_3 meet the requirements of migration of t_1. However, the migration from c_1 to c_2 costs 1.1s, while the migration from c_1 to c_3 only costs 1s. In this condition, we will select the second strategy as ms_1. Task t_2 only occupies one VM which c_4 can provide adequately. Thus we select c_4 as the migration target of t_2. After the two migration, the cloudlet c_1 is idle, and the set $\{ms_1, ms_2\}$ is denoted as mc_1.

We assume there are N cloudlets, i.e., $\{rs_1, rs_2, \ldots, rs_N\}$. A standby cloudlet set SPM is used to store the cloudlets which have idle space. Once a migration composition is generated, the full cloudlets shall be removed from SPM, and SPM shall be updated. We assume there are K migration compositions generated, i.e., $\{mc_1, mc_2, \ldots, mc_K\}$. Because the next migration composition is generated by iteration, the next migration composition need cover all the migration strategies in previous composition.

In Algorithm 1, we firstly sort the cloudlets in the decreasing order of idle VMs and create the standby cloudlet set which stores the cloudlets with idle space (Lines 1 to 7). Then we analyze each task, select the appropriate cloudlet to host all the VMs of the task and generate migration compositions (Lines 8 to 28).

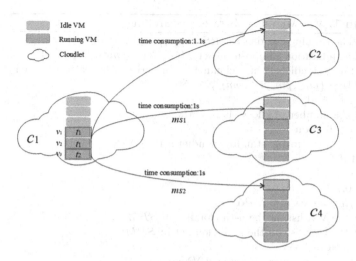

Fig. 3. An example of migration target selection

3.2 Multi-objective Optimization Scheduling

Algorithm 1 generates all the migration compositions which meet the requirements. Then in this section, the Simple Additive Weighting (SAW) and Multiple Criteria Decision Making (MCDM) techniques [12] are applied to multi-objective resource scheduling.

The SAW method is mainly used to calculate the weight of several criteria. The QoS criteria are divided into two categories, positive criterion and negative criterion. In this experiment, energy consumption and time consumption are both negative criteria whose quality decreases as its value increase. Algorithm 1 is designed to acquire the migration composition set MC. Each migration composition in MC brings about an energy consumption value and a time consumption value. Let $E_{All} = (E_{All}^i(t), 1 \leq i \leq K)$ be the energy consumption value and $T_{All} = (T_{All}^i(t), 1 \leq i \leq K)$ be the time consumption value. According to the specifications above, the utility value generated by migration is calculated by:

$$U_i(t) = \frac{E_{All}^{\max}(t) - E_{All}^i(t)}{E_{All}^{\max}(t) - E_{All}^{\min}(t)} \cdot w_E + \frac{T_{All}^{\max}(t) - T_{All}^i(t)}{T_{All}^{\max}(t) - T_{All}^{\min}(t)} \cdot w_T \quad (15)$$

In this formula, $E_{All}^{\max}$ and $E_{All}^{\min}$ represent the maximum and minimum energy consumption in all migration composition respectively. $T_{All}^{\max}$ and $T_{All}^{\min}$ represent the maximum and minimum time consumption in all composition respectively. w_E and w_T are the weight of energy consumption and the weight of time consumption.

With the formula above, the utility value of each migration composition can be calculated. The MCDM technique is mainly used to make the final determination in migration compositions. We select the composition with the maximum utility value as the final scheduling strategy. In addition, in order to save the

---

Algorithm 1. VM Migration Strategy Searching

Require: The running cloudlet set $RS = \{rs_1, rs_2, \ldots, rs_N\}$
Ensure: The migration composition set $MC = \{mc_1, mc_2, \ldots, mc_K\}$
1: Sort the cloudlets in cloudlets in the decreasing order of idle VMs, $PM = \{pm_1, pm_2, \ldots, pm_N\}$
2: **for** $n=1$ to N **do**
3:     Get the number of idle VMs in PM_n, i.e., c_n
4:     **if** $c_n > 0$ **then**
5:         Add pm_n to the standby cloudlet set, i.e., SP_M
6:     **end if**
7: **end for**
8: $flag = 0, n = 1$
9: **while** $flag = 0 \&\& n \leq N$ **do**
10:     Get the VM list on the n-th cloudlet in SPM
11:     Get the task list on the n-th cloudlet in SPM
12:     **for** each task **do**
13:         Get the number of occupied VMs
14:         Select the cloudlets with least idle space to host the VMs
15:         Calculate T_All for all selected cloudlets
16:     **end for**
17:     Generate a temporal strategy with smallest T_{All}
18:     **if** all the VMs can be migrated away **then**
19:         Generate a migration composition mc_n
20:         Add mc_n to MC
21:         Update the SPM
22:     **else**
23:         $flag = 1$
24:         Delete the temporal strategy
25:     **end if**
26:     $n = n + 1$
27: **end while**
28: **return** MC

---

energy consumption, we need to set the vacant cloudlets to the sleeping mode after finishing the migration.

In Algorithm 2, we firstly calculate energy consumption value and time consumption value of each migration composition (Lines 2 to 5). From them, we get the maximum and minimum value of both energy and time (Lines 6 to 7). Then we use the formula (15) to calculate the utility values of each migration composition (Lines 8 to 10). Finally, we select the best scheduling strategy and set all the vacant cloudlets to the sleeping mode (Lines 11 to 12).

4   Experiment Evaluation

In this section, a serious of comprehensive experiments are conducted to evaluate performance of our proposed balanced cloudlet management method for wireless

---

Algorithm 2. Multi-objective Optimization Scheduling

Require: The migration composition set MC
Ensure: VM scheduling strategy
 1: **for** each migration composition in MC **do**
 2:     Calculate the energy consumption value E_{All}
 3:     Calculate the time consumption value T_{All}
 4: **end for**
 5: Get maximum and minimum energy consumption values
 6: Get maximum and minimum time consumption values
 7: **for** each migration composition in MC **do**
 8:     Calculate the utility values
 9: **end for**
10: Schedule the VMs by the strategy with maximum utility value
11: Set the vacant cloudlets to the sleeping mode

---

metropolitan area network. In the process of comparison, the running state without migration is marked as a benchmark, our proposed method is abbreviated as BCM.

4.1 Experimental Context

In our experiment, HP ProLiant ML 110 G4 is selected as the cloudlet server to create the cloud infrastructure services network. Its basic configuration consists Intel Xeon 3040, Dual-Processor clocked at 1860 MHz and 4 GB of RAM. The baseline power of server, the baseline power of VM and the running power of VM are 86 W, 6 W and 4 W, respectively. Seven basic parameters and the range of values in this experiment are shown in Table 2. More specifically, 6 different-scale datasets are generated for our experiment, and the number of running cloudlets are 50, 100, 150, 200, 250 and 300, respectively.

4.2 Performance Evaluation

In this section, we analyze the energy consumption, resource utilization efficiency and transmission time consumption to validate our proposed method.

Energy Consumption Evaluation. In the experiment, the energy consumption here consists three parts, VM energy consumption, cloudlet energy consumption and transmission energy consumption. According to the experiment, about half of the cloudlets will be turn off after migrations. With the decrease of the number of running cloudlets, the cloudlet energy consumption will decrease, while the transmission energy consumption will increase. Figure 4 illustrates that BCM method saves 17.7%, 22.2%, 23.1%, 23.3%, 23.7% and 25.3% of energy when the number of cloudlets is 50, 100, 150, 200, 250 and 300, respectively. It can be concluded that the energy consumption in the BCM method is much less than the energy consumption in the benchmark case. To summary, our proposed BCM method can achieve the goal of saving energy.

Table 2. Parameter settings

Parameter	Domain
Number of running cloudlets	{50, 100, 150, 200, 250, 300}
Number of running VMs in each cloudlet	[1, 6]
Number of VMs on each cloudlet	6
Transmission rate between APs (Mb/s)	540
Transmission rate between AP and cloudlet (Mb/s)	1200
VM duration time	[1, 3]
VM transmission data (Gb)	[0.5, 0.8]

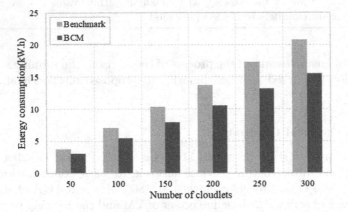

Fig. 4. Comparison of total energy consumption with Benchmark and BCM.

Resource Utilization Efficiency. Resource utilization efficiency is a dimension to calculate the average proportion of resources used in all cloudlets. As is shown in Fig. 5, the result illustrates that BCM method improves 28.3%, 40.0%, 35.3%, 33.7%, 39.7% and 43.1% of resource utilization efficiency when the number of cloudlets is 50, 100, 150, 200, 250 and 300, respectively. Stated thus, our proposed BCM method has much better resource utilization efficiency than benchmark case.

Transmission Delay Time. VM migrations between APs result in the time consumption, which has a negative impact on the performance. With the increase of the number of APs which VMs need to be migrated through, the time consumption will have a sharp growth. From Fig. 6, simulation results show that the average migration time consumption fluctuates around 3.8 s in the simulation environment.

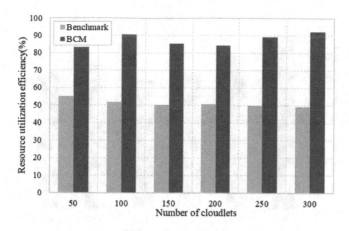

Fig. 5. Comparison of resource utilization efficiency with Benchmark and BCM.

5 Related Work

Recently, the growing market requirements of wireless broadband promotes the development of WMAN. Many advantages, such as fast speed and economical cost, make it popular among users. Nowadays, more and more complex applications are used in mobile devices, such as virtual reality, augmented reality, and interactive games. Due to the limitations of mobile device including battery, computing power, and CPU resources, users in urban cities intend to accomplish these tasks in cloud environment increasingly. However, the tremendous transmission delay is one significant limitation of migrating tasks to the remote clouds which is far away from mobile users [2,15]. In order to reduce the delay, cloudlets as a new technology, are deployed in WMAN [5]. Users can migrate computing-intensive tasks to the local cloudlets to achieve better user experience.

With the large-scale use of cloudlets, when the cloudlets are in the state of low load, the problems of energy consumption are often ignored. In other words, a cloudlet will waste a large quantities of energy if there are only few tasks executing on it. Therefore, it is necessary for us to find a optimal migration scheduling strategy.

To reduce the expected response time of migrating tasks to cloudlets, Li et al. [16] put forward a series of cloudlet server deployment issues in WMAN and proposed two novel cloudlet server deployment strategies, which achieve the goal of saving time by reducing the expected response time of the system. Liu et al. [17] proposed a cloudlet selection model based on mixed integer linear programming (MILP) and a resource allocation model based on MILP, in order to enable better performance in terms of access latency and resource utilization. Mudassar Ali et al. [18] proposed a delay minimization optimization problem under maximum workload and delay constraints. They formulated an optimization problem for joint cloudlet selection and latency minimization in fog network, and solved it with a distributed and self-organizing solution.

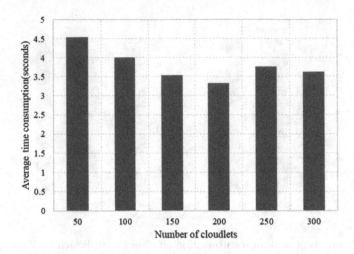

Fig. 6. Time consumption with BCM.

From the above analysis, it can be concluded that few investigations and studies have considered the joint optimization for both energy consumption and time consumption in cloudlet-based WMAN.

6   Conclusion and Future Work

In this paper, we formulated a problem for reducing energy consumption and time consumption in wireless metropolitan area network. In order to solve the challenge, a balanced cloudlet management method named BCM is proposed. In our method, the SAW and MCDM techniques are applied to optimize scheduling strategy. Finally, we carry out experiments to verify our proposed method.

For future work, we plan to apply our proposed method to real-world cloudlet-based WMAN and carry further investigation.

References

1. Baskaran, S.B.M., Raja, G.: Blind key distribution mechanism to secure wireless metropolitan area network. CSI Trans. ICT **4**(2–4), 1–7 (2016)
2. Yuan, C., Li, X., Wu, Q.M.J., Li, J., Sun, X.: Fingerprint liveness detection from different fingerprint materials using convolutional neural network and principal component analysis. Comput. Mater. Contin. **53**(4), 357–371 (2015)
3. Lo'ai, A.T., Bakheder, W., Song, H.: A mobile cloud computing model using the cloudlet scheme for big data applications. In: 2016 IEEE First International Conference on Connected Health: Applications, Systems and Engineering Technologies (CHASE), pp. 73–77. IEEE (2016)
4. Jin, A.-L., Song, W., Zhuang, W.: Auction-based resource allocation for sharing cloudlets in mobile cloud computing. IEEE Trans. Emerg. Top. Comput. **6**(1), 45–57 (2018)

5. Pang, Z., Sun, L., Wang, Z., Tian, E., Yang, S.: A survey of cloudlet based mobile computing. In: International Conference on Cloud Computing and Big Data, pp. 268–275 (2016)
6. Zhang, Y., Niyato, D., Wang, P.: Offloading in mobile cloudlet systems with intermittent connectivity. IEEE Trans. Mob. Comput. **14**(12), 2516–2529 (2015)
7. Chen, X., Jiao, L., Li, W., Fu, X.: Efficient multi-user computation offloading for mobile-edge cloud computing. IEEE/ACM Trans. Netw. **24**(5), 2795–2808 (2016)
8. Shen, J., Tan, H.-W., Wang, J., Wang, J.-W., Lee, S.-Y.: A novel routing protocol providing good transmission reliability in underwater sensor networks. 網際網路技術學刊 **16**(1), 171–178 (2015)
9. Pan, Z., Zhang, Y., Kwong, S.: Efficient motion and disparity estimation optimization for low complexity multiview video coding. IEEE Trans. Broadcast. **61**(2), 166–176 (2015)
10. Xiang, H., et al.: An adaptive cloudlet placement method for mobile applications over GPS big data. In: Global Communications Conference, pp. 1–6 (2017)
11. Dolui, K., Datta, S.K.: Comparison of edge computing implementations: fog computing, cloudlet and mobile edge computing. In: Global Internet of Things Summit (GIoTS), pp. 1–6. IEEE (2017)
12. Xu, X., Zhang, X., Khan, M., Dou, W., Xue, S., Yu, S.: A balanced virtual machine scheduling method for energy-performance trade-offs in cyber-physical cloud systems. Futur. Gener. Comput. Syst. (2017, in Press)
13. Garroppo, R.G., Nencioni, G., Procissi, G., Tavanti, L.: The impact of the access point power model on the energy-efficient management of infrastructured wireless lans. Comput. Netw. **94**, 99–111 (2016)
14. Xu, X., Dou, W., Zhang, X., Chen, J.: Enreal: An energy-aware resource allocation method for scientific workflow executions in cloud environment. IEEE Trans. Cloud Comput. **4**(2), 166–179 (2016)
15. Kaur, J., Kaur, K.: A fuzzy approach for an IoT-based automated employee performance appraisal. Comput. Mater. Contin. **53**(1), 24–38 (2015)
16. Li, D., Wu, J., Chang, W.: Efficient cloudlet deployment: local cooperation and regional proxy. In: 2018 International Conference on Computing, Networking and Communications (ICNC), pp. 757–761. IEEE (2018)
17. Liu, L., Fan, Q.: Resource allocation optimization based on mixed integer linear programming in the multi-cloudlet environment. IEEE Access **6**, 24533–24542 (2018)
18. Ali, M., Riaz, N., Ashraf, M.I., Qaisar, S., Naeem, M.: Joint cloudlet selection and latency minimization in fog networks. IEEE Trans. Ind. Inform. **PP**(99), 1–8 (2018)

Uncertainty Analytics and Formal Verification

Uncertainty Analysis of Rainfall Spatial Interpolation in Urban Small Area

Jie Huang[1], Changfeng Jing[2(✉)], Jiayun Fu[2], and Zejun Huang[1]

[1] School of Computer Science and Technology,
Hangzhou Dianzi University, Hangzhou 310018, China
[2] School of Geomatics and Urban Spatial Informatics,
Beijing University of Civil, Engineering and Architecture, Beijing 100044, China
jingcf@bucea.edu.cn

Abstract. Uncertainty analysis have attracted increasing attention of both theory and application over the last decades. Owing to the complex of surrounding, uncertainty analysis of rainfall in urban area is very little. Existing literatures on uncertainty analysis paid less attention on gauge density and rainfall intensity. Therefore, this study focuses on urban area, which a good complement to uncertainty research. In this study, gauge density was investigated with carefully selecting of gauge to covering evenly. Rainfall intensity data were extracted from one rainfall event at begin, summit and ending phases of rainfall process. Three traditional methods (Ordinary Kriging, RBF and IDW) and three machine methods (RF, ANN and SVM) were investigated for the uncertainty analysis. The result shows that (1) gauge density has important influence on the interpolation accuracy, and the higher gauge density means the higher accuracy. (2) The uncertainty is progressively stable with the increasing of rainfall intensity. (3) Geostatistic methods has better result than the IDW and RBF owing to considering spatial variability. The selected machine learning methods have good performance than traditional methods. However, the complex training processing and without spatial variability may reduce its practicability in modern flood management. Therefore, the combining of traditional methods and machine learning will be the good paradigm for spatial interpolation and uncertainty analysis.

Keywords: Rainfall · Spatial interpolation · Ordinary Kriging ·
Random forest · Machine learning

1 Introduction

Rainfall is one of the most important parameters for the flood management, such as hydrological models. Although some weather radars or satellite can get the short timely precipitation data, the ground rain gauge network is still the precise rainfall measure instruments, especially in the urban area. But at most situation it is with a sparse network [1]. Spatial interpolation had been widely used method to estimate the rainfall based on the gauge network, which has been a hot research issue. The common domains using spatial interpolation include meteorology [2], climate [3] and environment [4]. Three substantial roles of interpolation in meteorology domain include

H. Gao et al. (Eds.): TridentCom 2018, LNICST 270, pp. 79–95, 2019.
https://doi.org/10.1007/978-3-030-12971-2_5

parameter for hydrological model [5], area mean rainfall [6], simulating and mapping the rainfall map [7].

Understanding of the uncertainty of interpolation is vital for hydrological model or flood management. But there are only a very few researches on interpolation uncertainties [1]. Uncertainty is the one of challenge in modern flood management because the non-stationarity data come from multiple sources which raises new challenges for uncertainty analysis [8, 9]. Research on uncertainty focus on catchment such as estimating basin precipitation [10], uncertainty analysis for gauge network design within Folsom Lake watershed [11], assessment of precipitation spatiotemporal distribution for hydrological process simulation in the Three Gorges Basin [12]. Considering uncertainty factors, Elevation based topographic influence on spatial interpolation was validated [2]. Rainfall spatial variability is another important factor in interpolation, and its influence is investigated for the numerical simulation model [7].

In general, most of the existing research on uncertainty of rainfall interpolation suffer from several drawbacks. First, there is seldom researches in urban area. The probable causes is the spare gauge network which can bring bias and non-stationarity error [1]. In fact, it is necessary to estimate the uncertainty in urban areas because the precipitation patterns, climatology and surroundings in urban areas are quite different from those catchments [13, 14]. Furthermore, existing research lacks attention on gauge density and rainfall intensity. Existing research argues that rain gauge density is one of factor for the uncertainty [5]. However, owing to the spare gauge network in urban area, it is insufficient number for gauge density analysis [15, 16]. Rainfall intensity affects the measuring error of rain gauge and shows the spatial and temporal distribution of rainfall. Hence, it has also affected the interpolation uncertainty. As a result, the uncertainty of rainfall in urban area and its relationship to gauge density and rainfall intensity are worth of to further investigation.

In this paper, taking the aspects described above into consideration, we investigated the uncertainty with gauge density and rainfall intensity using various spatial interpolation including machine learning methods in urban area. Rain gauge network has 37 gauges, which is enough in number to validate the relationship of uncertainty and gauge density. The network is thoroughly designed based on rules for flood emergency management in dense population city [17]. Although many factors in uncertainty analysis such as rainfall variability, catchment size, topography, and the spatial interpolation technique [5], the topography and rainfall variability were excluded because on the most plain area in study area and data selected from one rainfall event. A 10% interval was adopted to select rain gauge representing different gauge density, meanwhile ensuring the even covering the whole area. Rainfall intensity data was carefully selection at the beginning, summit and ending phases of rainfall event. As for the interpolation methods, deterministic methods and geostatistic methods were both validated. In order to compare the intelligence of interpolation, three machine learning methods were also investigated.

The rest of our paper is organized as follows. Some interpolation methods and uncertainty analysis works are presented in Sect. 2. In Sect. 3, methods and measurements for uncertainty used in this paper are descripted. Following these methods, results are shown in Sect. 4. Validation on uncertainty with gauge density and rainfall intensity are discussed in Sect. 4. We conclude our work in Sect. 5.

2 Study Area and Related Work

2.1 Study Area

A case study in Xicheng District, Beijing, China is selected to investigate our research. It has a total area of approximately 50.7 km2 with about 1,259,000 inhabitants (in 2000 Census). Now, it has totally 37 rain gauges, which means one gauge evenly covering 1.37 km2. Figure 1 shows the study area and rain gauge network.

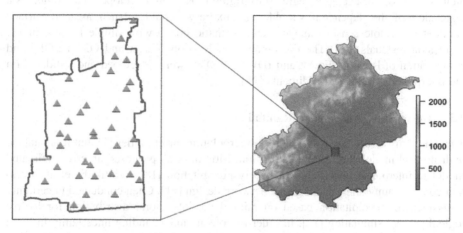

Fig. 1. Study are and rain gauge network.

2.2 Spatial Interpolation Methods

Rain gauge network is generally the first selection for precise measuring rainfall. However, its spare deployment needs various interpolation methods for accurate estimating. One of challenges lies in choosing the right interpolation [16, 18, 19]. The widely used classification of interpolation methods is two categories: deterministic and geostatistic methods [16]. According to complexity of methods, deterministic methods include arithmetic average, Thiessen polygon, Inverse Distance Weight (IDW) and polynomial interpolation [5]. Among them, IDW is the conspicuous method that gives the weight by the inverse of distance. Geostatistic methods such as Ordinary Kriging (OK) and its variants present estimation for un-sample points considering the spatial correlation of sample points [20]. Some literatures argue that geostatistic methods have more performance than deterministic method [21, 22], the other present the interpolation accuracy is case dependent [5, 16, 20]. Although some robust interpolation methods have been developed, such as Gaussian copulas [1], they are rarely used in rainfall interpolation due to their complexity and heavy data requirement.

Machine learning methods, such as random forest (RF) and support vector machine (SVM), have present their capability for accurate estimation at un-sample points. These methods can achieve good estimation even if there are noise data in sample points [23].

SVM has been applied to rainfall data in a previous study [24]. Machine learning methods (RF and SVM) have be investigated for spatial interpolation of environmental variables [25].

Either deterministic method or geostatistic method are found to be more case dependent and no one of these methods can carry perfect interpolation for all rainfall event [20]. Therefore, some combined methods are applied in rainfall prediction. Sometime, the combined method is called the third classification of interpolation methods [21, 25]. The combined schema can strength their advantages and minimized their weakness. For example, regression-kriging (RK) were developed that combines a regression of the dependent variable on auxiliary variables (such as land surface parameters, remote sensing imagery and thematic maps) with simple kriging of the regression residuals [26]. The combination of Random Forest and OK (RFOK) and combination of Random Forest and IDW (RFIDW) were developed and validated on the interpolation of seabed sediments [25].

2.3   Uncertainty Analysis on Rainfall

There are only a very few researches on interpolation uncertainties [1], but it is vital for hydrological model and rainfall estimation. Moulin et al. proposed an error estimated model to interpolate uncertainty of hourly precipitation [18]. Tsintikidis et al. investigated uncertainty analysis for gauge network design [11]. Chen conducted uncertainty assessment of precipitation based on rainfall spatiotemporal distribution for hydrological process simulation [12]. In order to holistic understanding uncertainty in flood management, a framework for uncertainty analysis to support decision making has been established [8]. In view of case study area, catchment and big space had been pay more attention, such as basin precipitation [10], Folsom Lake watershed in US [11], the Three Gorges Basin in China [12], and the upper Loire River in France covering 3234 km2 [18]. On the opposite, there is seldom research in urban area. Elevation and rainfall variability are the widely considered factor for uncertainty analysis. It has been validated that incorporating with elevation can improve the interpolation accuracy [2]. Incorporating the use of spatially-variable precipitation data from a long-range radar in the simulation of the severe flood, spatial variability can influent the total precipitated volumes, water depths and flooded areas [7]. In addition, research argues measurement error from rain gauge network is one of the main sources for uncertainty [5]. Gauge error includes error from device and gauge density in gauge network. In generally, the former had been calibrated in factory. But there is a little research on gauge density. In recent, Otieno conducted similar research in catchment covering 135 km2 with 49 gauges [16].

3   Methodology

3.1   Spatial Interpolation Methods

The general interpolation methods used in this study were Inverse Distance Weighting (IDW), Ordinary Kriging (OK) and Radial Basis Functions (RBF). The main software is the Geostatistical Analyst package of software ArcGIS developed by ESRI Inc. Furthermore, three machine learning methods were also investigated in this study to validate its' accuracy.

Inverse Distance Weighting (IDW). IDW interpolation method is established on the basis of the hypothesis that neighboring point has the more similar properties than the farther one. The principle of IDW methods shows that the estimated value of interpolation points is inversely proportion of the distance from known points [27, 28]. Therefore, it gives greater weights to points closest to the prediction location, and weights diminish as a function of distance. The formula as shown:

$$z(x) = \left[\sum_{i=1}^{n} \frac{z_i}{d_i^{\lambda}}\right] / \left[\sum_{i=1}^{n} \frac{1}{d_i^{\lambda}}\right] \tag{1}$$

Where $z(x)$ is the predicted value at an interpolated point, z_i is the ith sample point, n is the total number of sample points, d_i is the distance between the i sample point and the interpolated point, λ is the weighting power which may decide the weight affected by distance.

Ordinary Kriging (OK). Ordinary kriging is one of the most widely used stochastic interpolation methods (Webster and Oliver 2007), which has been engaged for estimating missing rainfall, areal rainfall distribution from point rainfall data, and data fusion of rain gauge and radar data [29, 30]. Kriging is an exact or smooth interpolation method depending on the measurement error model. Ordinary Kriging method is a widely used variant method that is closely relative to autocorrelation. The Kriging estimator is a linear combination of the observed values with weights that are derived from Kriging equations with semi variogram function. The parameters of the semi variogram function and the nugget effect can be estimated by an empirical semi variogram function. The semi variogram function is:

$$y(h) = \frac{1}{2N(h)} \sum_{i=1}^{N(h)} [z(x_i) - z(x_i + h)]^2 \tag{2}$$

Where $y(h)$ is the semi variance value at distance interval h; $N(h)$ is the number of sample pairs within the distance interval h; and $z(x_I + h)$ and $z(x_I)$ are sample values at two points separated by the distance interval h.

Radial Basis Functions (RBF). Radial basis function methods are a series of exact interpolation techniques, that is, the surface must pass through each measured sample point. They are special cases of splines. There are five different basis functions: tineplate spline, spline with tension, completely regularized spline, multi-quadric function, and inverse multi-quadric function [31]. In this study, we used the inverse multi-quadric function as the radial basis function. The prediction value by RBF can be expressed as the sum of two components [32]. The formula is:

$$z(x) = \sum_{i=1}^{m} a_i f_i(x) + \sum_{i=1}^{n} b_j h_j(d_j) \tag{3}$$

Where $h(d_j)$ shows the radial basis functions and d_j the distance from sample site to prediction point x, $f(x)$ is a trend function, a member of a basis for the space of polynomials of degree is less than m. The coefficients a_i and b_j are calculated by means of the resolution of the linear equations; m and n are the total number of known points used in the interpolation.

Machine Learning Methods. During the past several decades, machine learning methods have been extensively engaged in numerous fields of science and technology. Machine learning methods can train complex data to find a fit model with maximum accuracy and lowest complexity. In this study, three methods were investigated to validate rainfall interpolation accuracy, which include Random Forest (RF), Artificial Neural Network (ANN) and Support Vector Machine (SVM).

Random forest is an ensemble predictor with many tree models. Each tree model depends on the values of a sampled random vector respectively and under the same distribution for all trees in the forest [33]. The RF method can achieve higher predictive accuracy because a set of trees or networks have more robust abilities than one single tree [34], which has been used for data clear applications such as missed data prediction [35]. In addition, RF method has higher efficiency on large dataset with high dimension and easier to use without understanding the data distribution model. In this study, RF adopted the training rainfall data as regressive trees, then forming the forest. Each tree is independent from the others since a random predictor variable is prepared for each node.

The Artificial Neural Network (ANN) is famous on its capability to learn linear predictors from the complex nonlinear data by modeling the target variable using a hidden layer of variable [36]. The general multilayer ANN model is made of three or more neuronal layers: input layer, output layer and one or more intermediate or hidden layer for feature extraction [37]. ANN is a black-box and isn't support the monitoring of model processing. The mean squared error (MSE) is often acted as measure for stopping criterion at each training and validation iteration. If multiple networks are averaged, the approach is comparable to the idea of random forest.

The Support Vector Machine (SVM) is a group of supervised learning method for classification or regression problem based on statistic learning theory [38]. The performance of SVM depends on the kernel function and responding parameters. The radial basis function is one of the popular kernel functions for SVM that had been used for land cover classification [39].

3.2 Accuracy and Uncertainty Evaluation

The performance of rainfall value interpolation is assessed by cross validation with leave-one-out, which has been used in existing rainfall interpolation literatures [16, 30]. According to principles of cross validation with leave-one-out, one sample data of the dataset is temporarily excluded for interpolation and the estimated value of this point is interpolated using the remaining sample points. This step is then repeated until all the points are all "removed – estimated" in turn. The accuracy and uncertainty are evaluated by the measurements of Root Mean Square Error (RMSE) and Coefficient Variation (CV), respectively.

RMSE shows reliable indicator for the spatial interpolation, which has been considered as a preferred evaluation for many applications. RMSE has been widely used in rainfall interpolation and prediction [16, 40]. The equation is shown as follow:

$$RMSE = \sqrt{\frac{\sum_{i=1}^{n} [\hat{z}(s_i) - z(s_i)]^2}{n}} \tag{4}$$

Where $\hat{z}(s_i)$ shows the estimated value of point s_i, $z(s_i)$ is the true value of point s_i, n is the total number of points used in the validation.

RMSE is often used to evaluate how far the estimated value are from the true value. RMSE ranges from 0 to infinity, and the smaller of the RMSE means the better estimation of this sample point. RMSE is robust for the evaluation based on the same data, but it would not match the multiple datasets with different variability. In this paper, seven rainfall events with different rainfall intensity were used to evaluate the relationship of rainfall intensity and interpolation accuracy. Considering the variability in intensity, the coefficient of variation (CV) is employed to measure the uncertainty with intensity [5]. The equation is shown as below.

$$CV = \frac{standard\ deviation\ of\ predicted\ rainfall\ value}{predicted\ rainfall\ value} \tag{5}$$

According to the Leave-one-out cross validation, the predicted rainfall value is the mean of values comes from all iterate computations. Therefore, the CV is defined as the standard deviation (SD) divided by the predicted rainfall value. The CV indicates how large differences of estimated rainfall value to its true value tend to be in comparison to their average [41]. The main appeal of the CV is that it takes account on the variability of observe variable by using the mean value, which removes the proportional affection with standard deviation. The CV is therefore a standardization of the SD that allows comparison of variability dataset [42].

4 Result and Discussion

4.1 Gauge Density Experiment

Numerous studies have been done on the comparison of various interpolation methods under different circumstances such as rainfall intensity, spatial and temporal scales. However, rain gauge density is a wide across issue relate to cost, interpolation accuracy and reliability. The influence of rain gauge density on rainfall interpolation is worth of particular interest [16], which need more attention.

In this study, different number of rain gauges were selected representing the different rain gauge density. Then three commonly used interpolation methods (IDW, OK and RBF) were adopted for interpolation, cross validation methods used for accuracy evaluation. Inspiring the sample method for varying density in literature [16], we used 10% interval as the rule to determine the number. It is about 5, 7, 10, 14, 17, 20, 24, 27 and 31 points from all 37 rain gauges, which mean 10.10, 7.21, 5.05, 3.61, 2.97, 2.53, 2.10, 1.87, 1.63 km2 per gauge covering respectively. With the distribution of selected gauges, selection was carefully done ensuring that the selected gauges can still reasonably covered. Figure 2 shows the gauge distribution of partial density.

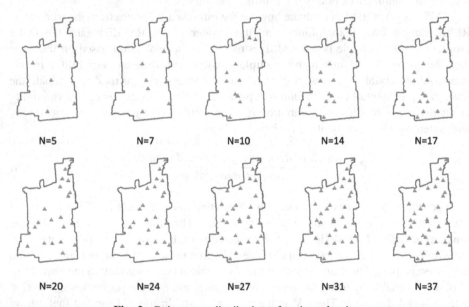

Fig. 2. Rain gauge distribution of various density.

Results were derived from the three interpolation methods, in where, the high quadric surface function is used in RBF methods. Table 1 gives the results. Figure 3 shows the trend graph of the result. Result shows the RMSE is unstable when the sample rate under 50%. Above 50%, it is the overall decreasing trend that is obvious along the increasing of gauge density and number among the three interpolation methods. The RMSE improved about 40%. Therefore, it can conclude that insufficient sample data may cause higher uncertainty and enough measurement is necessary for interpolation. The 50% sample ratio maybe a better threshold for good interpolation accuracy. It can also confirm in Otieno's research work [16]. However, more gauge density samples than Otieno's work (only 3 of 49 points) were tested in this paper. For the high RMSE with less points (such as 5 and 7 points) may has large uncertainty because the unstable error comes from rain gauge measuring error and rainfall variability. Rain gauge data are sensitive to wind and other surrounding environments [43]. The error caused by wind exposure and field is 2–10% for rainfall [44]. Other causes such as water splashing into and out of the collector, evaporation also have influence on measurements. Therefore, enough gauge is necessary for high accuracy interpolation.

Table 1. Rain gauge number and RMSE

Sample rate (rate/number)	RMSE of interpolation methods (mm)		
	IDW	OK	RBF
15/5	5.74	4.04	5.05
20/7	14.67	13.19	15.03
30/10	10.72	8.71	9.65
40/14	10.13	8.92	9.21
50/17	11.16	10.04	10.87
60/20	9.35	8.42	8.72
70/24	9.45	7.57	7.74
80/27	8.45	7.17	7.43
90/31	7.5	6.57	6.92

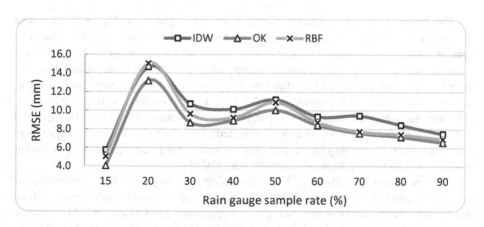

Fig. 3. The RMSE of varying gauge density.

4.2   Interpolation Uncertainty Against Rainfall Intensity

In addition to rainfall gauge network density, rainfall intensity is also of significant interest in urban hydrology as an important parameter for flood model and hydraulic infrastructure planning. Understanding uncertainty level would help for determining these parameters. Hence, the interpolation uncertainty against rainfall intensity is worth of investigation.

In order to reduce the rainfall variability influence, different rainfall intensity data are extracted from the same rainfall event. This study selected seven hourly rainfall data to achieve their rainfall intensity. The instant rainfall of all rain gauges at seven hours are collected to interpolation. The cross validation and CV represent the uncertainty. The description of intensity data is shown in Table 2. And Fig. 3 shows the value distribution of intensity. The intensity of 23rd hour has the maximum magnitude of intensity (Fig. 4).

Table 2. Intensity data of one rainfall event

No.	Time interval[a]	Average hourly intensity (mm/hour)	Instant average rainfall (mm)
1	22:00–23:00	9.41	9.42
2	23:00–24:00	6.37	15.79
3	6:00–7:00	16.82	52.52
4	9:00–10:00	15.08	70.56
5	13:00–14:00	2.63	76.93
6	15:00–16:00	0.77	78.72
7	16:00–17:00	1.17	79.89

[a]Day precipitation is between 20:00 yesterday and 20:00 today.

The scatter plot of CV against rainfall intensity is shown as Fig. 5. With seven intensity datasets and 37 gauges, 259 points are plotted by their intensity. The substantial decreasing trend is observed in this figure, which is similar to Muthusamy's result in literature [5]. In here, a general interpolation uncertainty is discussed, therefore there isn't the classification of rainfall intensity. Meanwhile, something can be drawn: (1) when the intensity <5.0 mm/h, the CVs have bigger deviation with some outliers; (2) when the intensity falling in [5.0, 10.0], the corresponding CVs range between 0.0 and 1.0. And the points are evenly distributed; (3) when the intensity bigger than 1.0 mm/h, the CVs are very stable and close to zero. This pattern is similar to existing research on relationship between intensity and CV [5].

After analyzed the all of 259 sample points, we explored the relationship of uncertainty and the various rainfall intensity at different phases of rainfall event. Three phases with seven datasets are picked up: beginning (23 o'clock and 24 o'clock), summit of rainfall process (7 o'clock and 10 o'clock) and ending phase (14 o'clock, 16 o'clock and 17 o'clock). The result is shown as Fig. 6.

The distribution trend of CV changes from substantial decreasing state (as shown in Fig. 6(a)) to a stable state with clustering distribution (as shown in Fig. 6(e) to (f)).

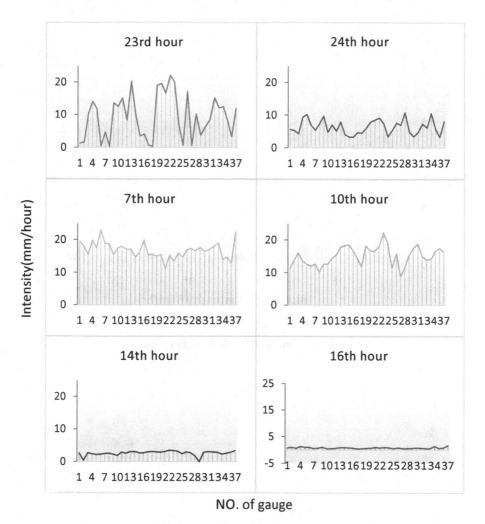

Fig. 4. Intensity value of selected.

In the 23 o'clock, the rain is beginning with large span of intensity (Fig. 6(a)), which is similar to Muthusamy's result in literature [5]. This decreasing trend is kept in the next hour, but these scatter points show discrete distribution (Fig. 6(b)). In the summit and ending phases of rainfall, the clustering distribution is strengthened. The CV value has changed from a big value to small one, which is from 6.0 of beginning phase (Fig. 6(a)) to 0.2 of ending phase (Fig. 6(e) to (g)).

The different average rainfall value means the bigger gap among CV. At begin, the rainfall value increased from zero and has a lower average rainfall with uneven distribution, then the higher CV maybe occurrence (Fig. 6(a)). On the opposite, at the ending phase, the bigger average rainfall value means the small Standard Deviation of rainfall, which brings a less amplitude of CV (Fig. 6(e) to (g)).

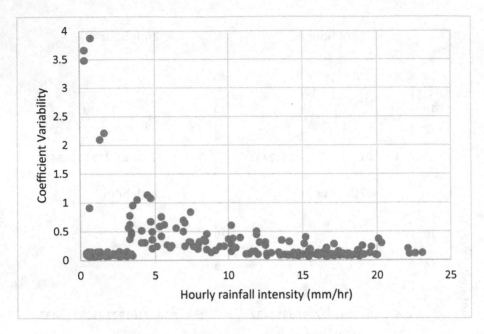

Fig. 5. Interpolation CV against rainfall intensity.

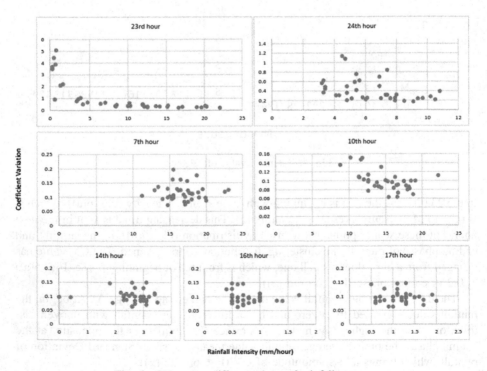

Fig. 6. CV against different phase of rainfall process

4.3   Interpolation Method Comparison

Spatial interpolation is generally estimating or predicting the value at un-sampled points. The mainstream methods can divided into two categories: deterministic and geostatistic methods [16]. The deterministic methods use the similarity and smoothness of surface as measurements for the interpolation to interpolate values. While the geostatistic methods utilize statistic methods and spatial correlation methods with the local variability or global variability theory [45]. Therefore, the geostatistic methods are capable of taking account of the spatial distribution of gauges and spatial variability of data. Therefore, Geostatistic methods has some advantage comparing to deterministic methods in theory. The widely used deterministic methods include IDW, RBF and Thiessen polygon [45]. Meanwhile, the Kriging and other variants such as Simple Kriging and Universal Kriging are the common geostatistic methods. These methods are validated in this paper. In addition, three machine learning methods were validated and compared with the main interpolations in this paper.

Four datasets were selected from one rainfall event at different time according to Table 2. The methods include OK, IDW and RBF with inverse multi-quadric function, RF, ANN and SVM were validated. The RMSE measurement of interpolation result are shown as Table 3.

Table 3.   RMSE of different methods

Method	RMSE (mm)			
	23rd hour	7th hour	16th hour	17th hour
OK	1.92	5.09	6.81	6.99
IDW	3.35	6.14	7.81	7.97
RBF	2.18	5.32	7.01	7.20
RF	1.94	4.05	5.33	5.47
ANN	2.14	4.92	5.73	5.85
SVM	2.05	4.05	5.49	5.52

The results demonstrate that all the interpolation methods can generate different interpolation accuracy because of the existing of uncertainty [6, 46]. According to the RMSE results from Table 3, OK was generally more accurate than IDW and RBF, which is a little different with Otieno's research [16] in which the IDW has better performance than OK method. Therefore, different data under different gauge network may achieve various result. Another probable cause is the input parameters for every interpolation method. Many studies argued that the input parameter of interpolation method is one of the important factors of uncertainty [47]. The validation of optimal power parameter of IDW was conducted by Otieno (2014), then more superior result was achieved. Generally, IDW and RBF need less and simple input parameters comparing to Kriging method. Although the more accurate result can get by carefully calibrating parameters of Kriging method, this is a dynamic parameter for different data.

Meanwhile, the machine learning methods have outstanding performance than traditional methods, which can be concluded from Table 3. The principle of machine learning may be able to explain this result. The training and fitting in machine learning can identify and remove the outlier or noise data for the hypothetic model. Therefore, the higher accuracy may be achieved. However, owing to the spatial variability of rainfall, some noise data in machine learning methods maybe the right value. So, the spatial variability of value should be considered and will be investigated in the future work.

Another criterion for selection interpolation method is the purpose of interpolation [32]. There are two main purposes of rainfall spatial interpolation: assessing the mean area rainfall and mapping the rainfall level. The former focuses on the overall trend of rainfall, and the latter cares of boundary of rainfall level with local max-min rainfall. IDW is very sensitive to weighting power, which is a function of inverse distance. This means that there is a higher influence or weight when closer to the center of the cell being estimated. RBF are based on the degree of smoothing across all sample points. Therefore, IDW methods keep the maximum and minimum value occurring at sample point, but it can generate at un-sample points in RBF method. Kriging method accounts for the spatial autocorrelation overall sample points and keeps the smooth of whole trend. In small area, owing to the weak spatial correlation and strong smoothing effect of kriging, the local maximum was underestimated and the local minimum was overestimated. Therefore, various methods are suitable for different purpose. When considering the overall trend, the Kriging method is more suitable, such as mapping rainfall distribution in study area. In contrast, IDW and RBF have the stronger ability to predict the local maximum and minimum and are suitable for interpolation to generate the rainfall level map.

5   Conclusion

Understanding of the uncertainty of interpolation is vital for flood management, which is the one of challenges in modern flood management. This paper carried out the uncertainty analysis on rainfall in urban area, which is a good complement work with the existing uncertainty analysis on catchment. This paper focus on influence comes from the gauge density and rainfall intensity. We carefully selected the gauge sample points with different number manually to our best to covering the study area. The rainfall intensity data comes from one rainfall event, which weakened the rainfall variability. Three traditional methods and three machine learning methods were selected for rainfall interpolation. We draw conclusions from our work: (1) the accuracy is largely improved with the increasing of gauge density. (2) The uncertainty is progressively stable with the increasing of rainfall intensity. In the hourly intensity, the decreasing of uncertainty with more range of intensity is more obvious than short range of intensity. (3) Interpolation method selection is a crucial thing to achieve accurate estimation according to interpolation purpose and rainfall intensity. Overall, the geostatistic methods has better performance than deterministic methods owing to considering spatial variability. But input parameters of geostatistic methods should carefully calibrate. The machine learning methods have better performance than traditional methods but without considering the spatial variability. In the future work, more combined methods with machine learning will be investigated, meanwhile, the spatial variability must be examined.

Acknowledgments. The authors would like to thank the valuable comments from anonymous reviewers. This study is jointly supported by the National Natural Science Foundation of China (Grant No. 41771412), the Beijing Natural Science Foundation (Grant No. 8182015), Beijing Advanced innovation center for future urban design (Grant No. X18052, X18058, X18158) and the Zhejiang Province Research Program (Grant No. 2015C33064).

References

1. Bárdossy, A., Pegram, G.: Interpolation of precipitation under topographic influence at different time scales. Water Resour. Res. **49**(8), 4545–4565 (2013)
2. Goovaerts, P.: Geostatistical approaches for incorporating elevation into the spatial interpolation of rainfall. J. Hydrol. **228**(1–2), 113–129 (2000)
3. Jeffrey, S.J., Carter, J.O., Moodie, K.B., Beswick, A.R.: Using spatial interpolation to construct a comprehensive archive of Australian climate data. Environ. Model Softw. **16**(4), 309–330 (2001)
4. Li, J., Heap, A.D.: Spatial interpolation methods applied in the environmental sciences: a review. Environ. Model Softw. **53**, 173–189 (2014)
5. Muthusamy, M., Schellart, A., Tait, S., Heuvelink, G.B.M.: Geostatistical upscaling of rain gauge data to support uncertainty analysis of lumped urban hydrological models. Hydrol. Earth Syst. Sci. **21**(2), 1077–1091 (2017)
6. Wagner, P.D., Fiener, P., Wilken, F., Kumar, S., Schneider, K.: Comparison and evaluation of spatial interpolation schemes for daily rainfall in data scarce regions. J. Hydrol. **464–465**, 388–400 (2012)
7. Courty, L., Rico-Ramirez, M., Pedrozo-Acuña, A.: The significance of the spatial variability of rainfall on the numerical simulation of urban floods. Water **10**(2), 207 (2018)
8. Hall, J., Solomatine, D.: A framework for uncertainty analysis in flood risk management decisions. Int. J. River Basin Manag. **6**(2), 85–98 (2008)
9. Hutter, G., Schanze, J.: Learning how to deal with uncertainty of flood risk in long-term planning. Int. J. River Basin Manag. **6**(2), 175–184 (2008)
10. Hrachowitz, M., Weiler, M.: Uncertainty of precipitation estimates caused by sparse gauging networks in a small. Mountainous Watershed. J. Hydrol. Eng. **16**(5), 460–471 (2011)
11. Tsintikidis, D., Georgakakos, K.R., Sperfslage, J.A., Smith, D.E., Carpenter, T.M.: Precipitation uncertainty and raingauge network design within Folsom Lake watershed. J. Hydrol. Eng. **7**(2), 175–184 (2002)
12. Cheng, M., et al.: Performance assessment of spatial interpolation of precipitation for hydrological process simulation in the Three Gorges Basin. Water **9**(11), 838 (2017)
13. Rupa, C., Mujumdar, P.P.: Quantification of uncertainty in spatial return levels of urban precipitation extremes. J. Hydrol. Eng. **23**(1), 04017053(2018)
14. Yang, L., Tian, F., Niyogi, D.: A need to revisit hydrologic responses to urbanization by incorporating the feedback on spatial rainfall patterns. Urban Clim. **12**, 128–140 (2015)
15. Liu, M., Bárdossy, A., Zehe, E.: Interaction of valleys and circulation patterns (CPs) on spatial precipitation patterns in southern Germany. Hydrol. Earth Syst. Sci. **17**(11), 4685–4699 (2013)

16. Otieno, H., Yang, J., Liu, W., Han, D.: Influence of rain gauge density on interpolation method selection. J. Hydrol. Eng. **19**(11), 04014024(2014)
17. Jing, C., Yu, J., Dai, P., Wei, H., Du, M.: Rule-based rain gauge network design in urban areas aided by spatial kernel density. Water Pract. Technol. **11**(1), 166–175 (2016)
18. Moulin, L., Gaume, E., Obled, C.: Uncertainties on mean areal precipitation: assessment and impact on streamflow simulations. Hydrol. Earth Syst. Sci. **13**(2), 99–114 (2009)
19. Kobold, M., Sušelj, K.: Precipitation forecasts and their uncertainty as input into hydrological models. Hydrol. Earth Syst. Sci. **9**(4), 322–332 (2005)
20. Ly, S., Charles, C., Degré, A.: Different methods for spatial interpolation of rainfall data for operational hydrology and hydrological modeling at watershed scale: a review. Base **17**(2), 392–406 (2013)
21. Li, J., Heap, A.D.: A review of comparative studies of spatial interpolation methods in environmental sciences: performance and impact factors. Ecol. Inform. **6**(3–4), 228–241 (2011)
22. de Amorim Borges, P., Franke, J., da Anunciação, Y.M.T., Weiss, H., Bernhofer, C.: Comparison of spatial interpolation methods for the estimation of precipitation distribution in Distrito Federal, Brazil. Theor. Appl. Climatol. **123**(1–2), 335–348 (2016)
23. Appelhans, T., Mwangomo, E., Hardy, D.R., Hemp, A., Nauss, T.: Evaluating machine learning approaches for the interpolation of monthly air temperature at Mt. Kilimanjaro, Tanzania. Spat. Stat. **14**, 91–113 (2015)
24. Gilardi, S., Begio, N.: Local machine learning models for spatial data analysis. J. Geogr. Inf. Decis. Anal. **4**(EPFL-ARTICLE-82651), 11–28 (2000)
25. Li, J., Heap, A.D., Potter, A., Daniell, J.J.: Application of machine learning methods to spatial interpolation of environmental variables. Environ. Model Softw. **26**(12), 1647–1659 (2011)
26. Hengl, T., Heuvelink, G.B.M., Rossiter, D.G.: About regression-Kriging: from equations to case studies. Comput. Geosci. **33**(10), 1301–1315 (2007)
27. Bhargava, N., Bhargava, R., Tanwar, P.S., Narooka, P.C.: Comparative study of inverse power of IDW interpolation method in inherent error analysis of aspect variable. In: Mishra, D., Nayak, M., Joshi, A. (eds.) Information and Communication Technology for Sustainable Development, pp. 521–529. Springer, Singapore (2018). https://doi.org/10.1007/978-981-10-3920-1_52
28. Maciej, T.: Spatial interpolation and its uncertainty using automated anisotropic inverse distance weighting (IDW) - cross-validation/Jackknife approach. J. Geogr. Inf. Decis. Anal. **2**(2), 18–30 (1998)
29. Adhikary, S.K., Muttil, N., Yilmaz, A.G.: Genetic programming-based Ordinary Kriging for spatial interpolation of rainfall. J. Hydrol. Eng. **21**(2), 1–14 (2016)
30. Berndt, C., Rabiei, E., Haberlandt, U.: Geostatistical merging of rain gauge and radar data for high temporal resolutions and various station density scenarios. J. Hydrol. **508**, 88–101 (2014)
31. ESRI: How radial basis functions work (2013)
32. Xie, Y., et al.: Spatial distribution of soil heavy metal pollution estimated by different interpolation methods: accuracy and uncertainty analysis. Chemosphere **82**(3), 468–476 (2011)
33. Breiman, L.: Random forests. Mach. Learn. **45**(1), 5–32 (2001)
34. Genuer, R., Poggi, J.M., Tuleau-Malot, C., Villa-Vialaneix, N.: Random forests for big data. Big Data Res. **9**, 28–46 (2017)
35. Kühnlein, M., Appelhans, T., Thies, B., Nauss, T.: Improving the accuracy of rainfall rates from optical satellite sensors with machine learning - a random forests-based approach applied to MSG SEVIRI. Remote Sens. Environ. **141**, 129–143 (2014)

36. Basheer, I.A., Hajmeer, M.: Artificial neural networks: fundamentals, computing, design, and application. J. Microbiol. Methods **43**(1), 3–31 (2000)
37. Prasad, R., Deo, R.C., Li, Y., Maraseni, T.: Input selection and performance optimization of ANN-based streamflow forecasts in the drought-prone Murray Darling Basin region using IIS and MODWT algorithm. Atmos. Res. **197**, 42–63 (2017)
38. Cortes, C., Cortes, C., Vapnik, V., Vapnik, V.: Support vector networks. Mach. Learn. **20**(3), 273–297 (1995)
39. Kavzoglu, T., Colkesen, I.: A kernel functions analysis for support vector machines for land cover classification. Int. J. Appl. Earth Obs. Geoinf. **11**(5), 352–359 (2009)
40. Sadler, J.M., Goodall, J.L., Morsy, M.M.: Effect of rain gauge proximity on rainfall estimation for problematic urban coastal watersheds in Virginia Beach, Virginia. J. Hydrol. Eng. **22**(9), 04017036(2017)
41. Cox, J.C., Sadiraj, V.: On the coefficient of variation as a measure of risk sensitivity. SSRN **3** (3), (2011)
42. Reed, G.F., Lynn, F., Meade, B.D.: Quantitative assays. Clin. Diagn. Lab. Immunol. **9**(6), 1235–1239 (2002)
43. Cristiano, E., Veldhuis, M.-C., Van De Giesen, N.: Spatial and temporal variability of rainfall and their effects on hydrological response in urban areas-a review. Hydrol. Earth Syst. Sci. **21**, 3859–3878 (2017)
44. WMO: Guide to Meteorological Instruments and Methods of observation (WMO-No.8), Seven edit. Geneva, Switzerland (2008)
45. Goovaerts, P.: Geostatistics in soil science: state-of-the-art and perspectives. Geoderma **89** (1–2), 1–45 (1999)
46. Ma, L., Chi, X., Zuo, C.: Evaluation of interpolation models for rainfall erosivity on a large scale. In: First International Conference on Agro-Geoinformatics (Agro-Geoinformatics), pp. 1–5. IEEE, Shanghai (2012)
47. Zhang, P., Liu, R., Bao, Y., Wang, J., Yu, W., Shen, Z.: Uncertainty of SWAT model at different DEM resolutions in a large mountainous watershed. Water Res. **53**, 132–144 (2014)

Automated and Optimized Formal Approach to Verify SDN Access-Control Misconfigurations

Amina Saâdaoui$^{(\boxtimes)}$, Nihel Ben Youssef Ben Souayeh, and Adel Bouhoula

Digital Security Research Lab, Sup'Com, University of Carthage, Tunis, Tunisia
{amina.saadaoui,nihel.benyoussef,adel.bouhoula}@supcom.tn

Abstract. Software-Defined Networking (SDN) brings a significant flexibility and visibility to networking, but at the same time creates new security challenges. SDN allows networks to keep pace with the speed of change by facilitating frequent modifications to the network configuration. However, these changes may introduce misconfigurations by writing inconsistent rules for Flow-tables. Misconfigurations can arise also between firewalls and Flow-tables in OpenFlow-based networks. Problems arising from these misconfigurations are common and have dramatic consequences for networks operations. Therefore, there is a need of automatic methods to detect and fix these misconfigurations. Given these issues, some methods have been proposed. Though these methods are useful for managing Flow-tables rules, they still have limitations in term of low granularity level and the lack of precise details of analyzed flow entries. To address these challenges, we present in this paper a formal approach that allows to discover Flow-tables misconfigurations using inference systems. The contributions of our work are the following: automatically identifying Flow-tables anomalies, using the Firewall to bring out real misconfigurations and proposing automatic method to deal with set-field action of flow entries.

These techniques have been implemented and we proved the correctness of our method and demonstrated its applicability and scalability. The first results we obtained are very promising.

Keywords: Flow entries · Flow table · SDN · Misconfigurations ·
FtDD · Inference system · Direct path · Firewall

1 Introduction

In SDN Network, devices can be programmed via different communication protocols, such as OpenFlow. In fact an openFlow network consists of a distributed collection of switches managed by a program running on a logically-centralized controller. Each switch has a flow table that stores a list of rules for processing packets. Each rule consists of a pattern (matching on packet header fields) and

H. Gao et al. (Eds.): TridentCom 2018, LNICST 270, pp. 96–112, 2019.
https://doi.org/10.1007/978-3-030-12971-2_6

actions (such as forwarding, dropping, modifying the packets, or sending them to the controller). The OpenFlow controller installs or uninstalls rules in the switches, reads traffic statistics, and responds to events. For each event, the controller program defines a handler, which may install rules or issue requests for traffic statistics. Therefore, Open flow and Software-Defined Networking (SDN) can simplify network management by offering programmers network-wide visibility and direct control over the underlying switches from a logically-centralized controller, but at the same time brings new security challenges by raising risks of software faults (or bugs), especially switches misconfigurations. Since companies rely only on the availability of their networks, such misconfigurations are costly. Due to the magnitude of this problem, our goal is to develop a method that allows to automatically identify configuration errors among the set of switches rules which should be well configured with respect to the firewall configuration. This task is challenging due to a number of reasons. First of all, an openflow switch generally comprises thousands of flow entries that are dependent and second flow entries do not always exactly match firewall rules. As an example, consider an enterprise network shown in Fig. 1. We have three switches their configurations are shown in Fig. 3. The firewall configuration that should be implemented is shown in Fig. 2 This example is considered throughout this paper to evaluate our approach to discover flow entries misconfigurations. We can note that the second flow entry fe_2, shown in Switch $S1$, is configured to forward traffic from the machine 172.27.2.3, to switch $S2$ and from this switch traffic will be forwarded to switch $S3$ using flow entry fe_2, then from the switch S_3 this traffic will be dropped using the flow entry fe_6, which is not conform to the requirements of the firewall configuration shown in Fig. 2 (rule r_2 will accept traffic from this source address). Although a misconfiguration is identified between these flow entries, most related studies [1,3,4] did not consider these configuration errors, also, most of these studies did not handle different actions of flow entries, precisely, the action set-Field that allow to modify header packet fields which can influence the path parsed by some packets and consequently the process of detection of misconfigurations. This task is more complex than it appears at first glance especially when a large number of switches and flow entries is deployed.

In this paper, we propose a new approach to discover misconfigurations in real-case openFlow switches configurations already designed, by considering all relations between all flow entries and all possible paths parsed by packets in a given Network. Our approach takes advantages of the interdependency of flow entries modeling their relations in a Flowtable decision diagram (FtDD). Our proposed method could be used also before updates occurred by the controller to verify if changes will induce further misconfigurations. This paper is organized as follows: Sect. 2 presents a summary of related work. Section 3 overviews the formal representation of flow entries, firewall configurations and details $FtDD$ structure. In Sect. 4, we present our inference systems to discover misconfigurations. In Sect. 5, we present first a study of the complexity of our inference systems, and then we address the implementation and evaluations of our tool. Finally, we present our conclusions and discuss our plans for future work.

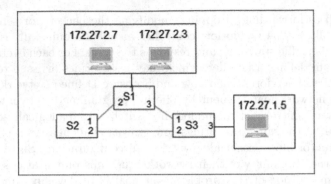

Fig. 1. Network topology

Rule N°	Source	Destination	Port	Action
1	172.27.2.7	172.27.1.5	80	drop
2	172.27.2.0/24	*	*	accept
3	172.27.1.5	*	*	accept
4	*	*	*	drop

Fig. 2. Firewall configuration

Switch1 Configuration

FE N°	Source	Destination	Port	Action
1	*	172.27.1.5	*	Fwd(S3)
2	172.27.2.3	*	*	Fwd(S2)
3	172.27.2.7	*	*	Fwd(S2)
4	172.2.3.7	*	*	Fwd(S3)
5	*	*	*	drop

Switch2 configuration

FE N°	Source	Destination	Port	Action
1	172.27.1.5	*	*	Set-Srce(172.27.1.5,172.27.2.7) && Fwd(S1)
2	172.27.2.0/24	*	*	Fwd(S3)
3	172.27.1.5	*	*	Fwd(S3)
4	172.27.3.7	*	*	Fwd(S3)
5	*	*	*	drop

Switch3 configuration

FE N°	Source	Destination	Port	Action
1	172.27.2.7	172.27.1.5	*	Fwd(port 3)
2	172.27.1.5	172.27.2.7	*	Fwd-Firewall
3	172.27.1.5	*	*	Fwd(S2)
4	172.27.2.3	172.27.1.5	*	drop
5	172.27.3.7	*	*	Fwd(S2)
6	*	*	*	drop

Fig. 3. Switches configurations

2   Related Work

A significant amount of research has addressed configurations analysis and modeling. For example, Some research has focused on firewall misconfiguration detection anad correction ([1,11,17,18]). Also, there was a considerable amount of work on detecting misconfiguration in routing ([2,7,10]). The concept of Open-Flow switch was introduced in [16] and used in different applications. The work done on OpenFlow switches did not address the problems of switches misconfiguration detection and correction; instead, recently, there have been many verification tools proposed for SDN. Some tools debug controller software or applications, while others check the correctness of network policies.

Controller software or applications verification: In [4] authors propose a tool named NICE which automates the testing of OpenFlow Apps. In fact it allows to find bugs in real applications and to test the atomic execution of system events. But this tool does not guarantee the errors absence and does not allow to check safety properties. Ball et al. propose another tool in [3] named Verifcon that allows to verify the correctness of SDN applications on a large range of topologies and sequences of network events. The limitation of this work is that authors focus on safety properties without verifying the liveness properties of packets (packets must eventually reach their destinations) and also they assume that events are executed atomically ignoring out-of order rule installations.

Network policies verification: Frenetic [8] is a domain-specific language for OpenFlow that aims to eradicate a large class of programming faults. Using Frenetic requires the network programmer to learn extensions to Python to support the higher-layer abstractions. OFRewind [19] enables recording and replay of events for troubleshooting problems in production networks due to closed-source network devices. However, it does not automate the testing of OpenFlow controller programs. Kazemian et al. [12] proposed a method that allows to verify network properties like reachability, by using Header Space Analysis HAS but their work does not allow to check in real-time if network policy still not violated after rules update for example. Netplumber presented in [12] uses a set of policies and invariants to do real time checking. It leverages header space analysis and keeps a dependency graph between rules but it does not allow to model dynamic network behaviors. Hu et al. introduced in [11] Flowgard a new tool that allows to verify the network policy by providing methods to detect and correct firewall policy violations in OpenFlow based networks. FlowChecker [1] applies symbolic model checking techniques on a manually-constructed network model based on binary decision diagrams to detect misconfigurations in Open-Flow forwarding tables. In [13] authors present a tool *VeriFlow* used for verifying network correctness before the rules and logic are implemented in the network devices. The tool will check the changes made to the network for correctness or anomalies before allowing the changes to be deployed. But when large changes in the network happen, VeriFlow is unable to keep up and it is necessary to allow rules to be installed without verification. Instead, the verification process will run in parallel, at the same time as the rules are installed.

The objectives of our work are different. We aim first to automatically identify Flow-tables anomalies, using the Firewall to bring out real misconfigurations and finally, we propose automatic method to deal with set-field action of flow entries. Proving the correctness and completeness of proposed techniques is an unavoidable step. Nevertheless, most existing studies and algorithm ignore to prove these two properties. In our work, by using formal representation and inference systems we proved their completeness and correctness.

3   Formal Specification

Our objective is to discover each misconfiguration with the minimum number of operations. Therefore, we need a formal specification to deal with this problem and also to prove the correctness and completeness of our work. In what follow, we define, formally, some key notions.

3.1   Open Flow Switch Flow Entries

An OpenFlow Switch configuration consists of a flow table, which perform packet lookups and forwarding, and an OpenFlow channel to an external controller. The switch communicates with the controller and the controller manages the switch via the OpenFlow protocol. A flow table contains a set of flow entries of the form $FL = \{fe_i => a_i; 1 =< i <= n\}$; each flow entry consists of match fields fe_i, and a set of actions to apply to matching packets $ai = \{FORWARD, CONTROLLER, set(field1, field2) \ and \ FORWARD, drop\}$, where the action $CONTROLLER$ allows to forward packets to the controller which will filter them using the firewall configuration.

3.2   Firewall Configuration

We consider a finite domain $\mathcal{P}$ containing all the headers of packets possibly incoming to or outgoing from a network.

A simple firewall configuration is a finite sequence of filtering rules of the form $FR = (r_i \Rightarrow A_i)_{0<i<N+1}$. These rules are tried in order, up to the first matching one. A filtering rule consists of a precondition r_i which is a region of the packet's space, usually, consisting of source address, destination address, protocol and destination port. Each right member A_i of a rule of FR is an action defining the behavior of the firewall on filtered packets: $A_i \in \{accept, deny\}$.

3.3   *FtDD* (Flow Table Decision Diagram) of a Path in a Distributed Environment

A flow tables decision diagram of our network, is constructed using the collection of flow entries of different flow tables of different switches in our network switches. Therefore, the $FtDD$ of our network could be represented as follows: $FtDD = \{dp_j; 1 <= j <= m\}$, which is an acyclic and directed graph that has the following properties: There is exactly one node in $FtDD$ that has no incoming edges. This node is called the root of $FtDD_i$. The nodes in $FtDD$ that have no outgoing edges are called terminal nodes. $FtDD_i$ is the union of direct paths dpi. The algorithm used to construct an $FtDD$ is detailed in [9,15]. Each direct path is represented as follows: $FtDD = \bigcup_{j(i:1 \to m)} dp_i.\ dp_j = dp_j.srce \wedge dp_j.protocol \wedge$ $dp_j.dest \wedge dp_j.flowEntries \wedge dp_j.action$. Where:

- $dp_j.srce$ is the range of source address represents by the direct path dp_j.
- $dp_j.dest$ is the range of destination address represents by the direct path dp_j.
- $dp_j.protocol$ is the range of protocols represented by the direct path dp_j.
- $dp_j.flowEntries$ is the set of flow entries from the flow table configuration that match the domain of packets represented by this direct path. But we have to precise for each rule the flow table that belongs to it.
- $dp_j.action= $ = the action of this direct path dp_j. The action of each direct path depends on the actions of each flow entry handled by this direct path from each switches in this path, so we have:
  - $dpj.action = accept$ if all flow entries applied the action forward from the source to the destination.
  - $dpj.action = drop$ if at least one rule applies the action drop to the packets handled by this direct path.
  - $dpj.action = set - Field(field1, field2)\ and\ Fwd(Sk)$ if in this direct path we have a flow entry that apply this action.
  - $dpj.action = Loop$, if the flow handled by this direct path is returned to a switch already exists in the set $dpj.flowEntries$.
  - $dpj.action = CONTROLLER$ if at least one rule applies this action to the packets matched by this direct path, packets forwarded to the controller will be handled by the firewall.

Our current work allows to automatically discover misconfigurations in all switches of our network by considering all relations between all flow entries and by considering also all parsed paths by using $FtDD$. In the next section we discuss our approach to deal with this problematic.

4   Inference Systems

In this work, our goal is to propose an automatic method that supports OpenFlow controller by effectively managing flow-tables entries in dynamic OpenFlow-based networks. To achieve our goal and address this challenge, we seek a solution based of inference systems.

4.1   Inference System for Constructing $FtDD$

The first step is to define a set In-switches composed by couples (S_{in}, I) switches from which the traffic flow first. Where I is source addresses that are linked to the switch S_{in}. The verification in our work is based on firewall requirements; therefore, we use the firewall rules and the network topology to define this set I. Our goal is to construct the $FtDD$. To achieve this goal we propose in Fig. 4 an inference system that presents steps to construct this $FtDD$.

$$Init \quad \overline{\varnothing, S_{in}, \varnothing, \varnothing}$$

$$Start \quad \frac{FtDD, \{fe\} \cup S_{in}, \varnothing, \varnothing}{construct_{FtDD}(FtDD, \{fe\} \cap I), S_{in}, FE_m, \varnothing} \quad \begin{array}{l} if(\{fe\} \cap I \neq \varnothing \ and \ fe.action = Fwd(S_j)) \\ where \ FE_m = \{(fe_m, dp) \ where \ (\{fe_m\} \in S_j \ and \\ \qquad\qquad dp = \{fe_m\} \cap \{fe\} \cap I) \ if \ \{fe_m\} \cap \{fe\} \cap I \neq \varnothing\} \end{array}$$

$$Pass \quad \frac{FtDD, \{fe\} \cup S_{in}, \varnothing, \varnothing,}{FtDD, S_{in}, \varnothing, \varnothing} \quad if \ no \ other \ rule \ applies$$

$$Apply \frac{FtDD, S_{in}, (fe_m, dp) \cup FE_m, F}{construct_{FtDD}(FtDD, dp), S_{in}, FE'_m, F'} \quad \begin{array}{l} if(dom(dp) \setminus F \neq \varnothing) \\ where \begin{cases} F' = dom(fe_m) \cup F \ if(verify\_Sw(fe_m, F)) \wedge F' = \varnothing \ otherwise \ \wedge \\ FE'_m = FE_m \cup \{(fe_n, fe_n \cap dp) \ where \ condition\_add\}\} \end{cases} \end{array}$$

$$Pass_{Apply} \frac{FtDD, S_{in}, (fe_m, dp) \cup FE_m, F}{construct_{FtDD}(FtDD, dp), S_{in}, FE_m, F} \quad if \ apply \ is \ not \ applied$$

$$Stop \frac{FtDD, \varnothing, \varnothing, \varnothing}{FtDD}$$

Fig. 4. Inference system for constructing FtDD

The rules of this inference system apply to quadruple $(ftdd, S_{in}, FE_m, F)$ where $ftdd$ is the Flow entries decision diagram of the couple (S_{in}, I), FE_m is a temporary variable contains a set of flow entries from different switches in our network that we should parse to get the real path from which packets from sources in the set I passed. F is a temporary variable contains the set of packet matched by rules already parsed. The inference rule $start$ allows to parse rules from the switch S_{in} that match the set I, this inference rule allows also to define the set FE_m if the action of the parsed flow entry fe is forward to another switch S_j, therefore this set contains rules from the switch S_j that match the set of packets matched by previous traffic. The rule apply allow to route all traffic according to rules matched and actions $FORWARD$. So the idea implemented by this inference system is as follows: For each flow entry from the switch S_{in}, we verify if its action is to forward to another switch, in this case, we parse flow entries of the new switch until we obtain a flow entry with an action drop, $CONTROLLER$ or a forward to another switch already parsed. Therefore, the condition to add a flow entry to the set of rules to be parsed is described, as follows:

The rule $Stop$ is applied when we parse and update all the paths of the set S_{in} (Fig. 5).

$$condition\_add = \begin{cases} fe_n.action = Fwd(S_k) \wedge fe_n \in S_k \wedge \\ (fe_n \cap dp \neq \varnothing) \wedge S_k \notin switches(dp) \end{cases}$$

Fig. 5. ConditionAdd

The function $Construct\_FDD$ is the function used to construct FDD depicted in previous work [9,15]. The flow entries decision diagram of all sets S_{in} is defined as follows: $FtDD = \bigcup ftdd$.

For example if we consider the network topology shown in Fig. 1, we should first start by defining possible inputs I_{in}. We have three sets of possible input addresses:

- $I1 = \{172.27.2.7, 172.27.2.3\}$ which is linked to switch S_1.
- $I2 = \{172.27.1.5\}$ which is linked to switch S_3.
- $I3 = \{*/I1UI2\}$ which is the set of possible input address sources that could income to switch S_2.

We have three sets of possible input address sources. By applying inference system shown in Fig. 4. We will obtain $FtDD$ shown in Figs. 6, 7 and 8 respectively.

In order to prove the correctness and completeness of our approach, we start by the following theorem:

- **Theorem** if $(\emptyset, S_{in}, \emptyset, \emptyset) \vdash^* FtDD$ then, $FtDD$ is correct and complete.
- **Proof** if $(\emptyset, S_{in}, \emptyset, \emptyset) \vdash^* FtDD$ then, $\forall p \in dom(I), \exists dp_i \in FtDD$ where $p \in dom(dp_i)$, because at each Flow table, there is a default flow entry that match all possible packets. Therefore, a packet will match at least on flow entry. Therefore, $FtDD$ is complete. If $(\emptyset, S_{in}, \emptyset, \emptyset) \vdash^* FtDD$, then $\forall p \in dp_i$, $dp_i.FlowEntries$ contains the path parsed by the packet p. In fact, at each step, and if the flow entry match the packet p, and this flow entry is not masked by previous traffic (the set F in our inference system), then one of the inference rules $Apply$ or $Start$ is applied, and these inference rules will apply

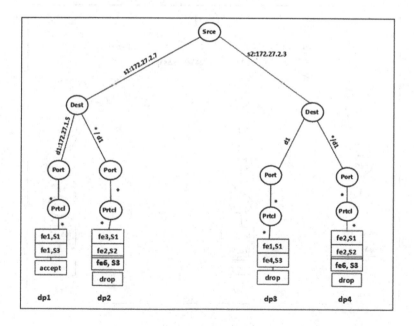

Fig. 6. FtDD of I1

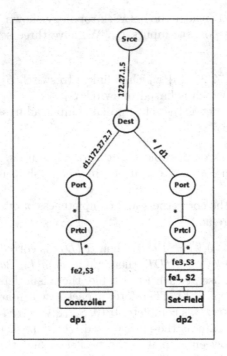

Fig. 7. FtDD of I2

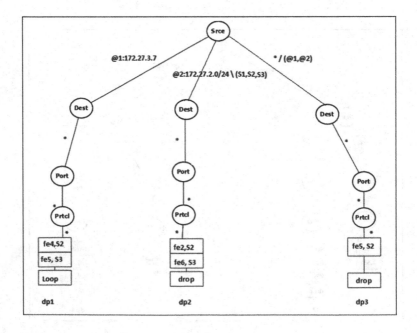

Fig. 8. FtDD of I3

the function $Construct_F DD$ which will add the flow entry applied to the direct path $dp_i.FlowEntries$. Therefore, $dp_i.FlowEntries$ contains exactly all flow entries parsed by the packet p. Then, $dp_i.FlowEntries$ is equivalent to the SDN path of the packet p. Therefore, our $FtDD$ is correct.

4.2   Inference System for Dealing with Set-Field Actions

For a flow entry, we must consider various Set-Field actions, which can rewrite the values of respective header fields in packets that can affect the process of verification. Therefore, before constructing $FtDD$ we have to analyze the impact of these modifications on the flow entries.

The inference system shown in Fig. 9 allows to find and assign effective actions to direct paths that have the action set-field.

In our work we are interested in discovering switches misconfigurations; therefore, knowing the effective action applied on each direct path is an unavoidable step. Our inference system is applied on four variables (shown in Fig. 9), The first one is the set $DP - Set$ which contains all direct paths in our $FtDD$ where actions of these direct paths is equal to "Set-Field(Field1, Field2) and Forward(Sk)": $DP - et = \{dp \in FtDD, dp.action = Set - Field(Field1, Field2) \land Forward(Sk)\}$. We should find the real action applied by these direct paths. The second one is our $FtDD$ constructed using the inference system defined in the previous section. The Third component dp_match contains all direct paths from $FtDD$ that match the same packets as a given direct path. The main inference rule in this inference system is $update\_FtDD$, it allows to update $Ftdd$ by assigning the effective action applied a given direct path. In fact, for each direct path from the set DP-Set we try to find this action by verifying if direct path that match the modified direct path (i.e., we modify field1 by field2) and have the switch S_k in their path (dp.flowEntries contains a flow entry from the switch S_k) have all the same action, if it is the case we assign this effective action to the direct path otherwise we consider the action as **UNDEFINED** (This indicative will help us to find misconfigurations in the next steps of our work). We have to precise that the new direct paths of our set Dp-match could contain other

$$Init\frac{}{DP_{Set}, FtDD, \varnothing, \varnothing}$$

$$Parse\frac{dp_{set} \cup DP_{Set}, FtDD, \varnothing, \varnothing}{DP_{Set}, FtDD, dp_{set}, DP_{match}} \quad where\ DP_{match} = \{dp \in FtDD\ where\ dp \cap modify - Field(dp_{set}) \neq \varnothing \land S_k \in dp.flowEntries\}$$

$$Update - FtDD\frac{DP_{Set}, FtDD, dp_{set}, DP_{match}}{DP_{Set}, FtDD', \varnothing, \varnothing} \quad if(\forall dp \in DP_{match}\ dp.action \neq set - Field(f1, f2))$$
$$where\ FtDD' = set - action(FtDD, dp_{set}, Action(DP_{match}))$$

$$Pass\frac{DP_{Set}, FtDD, dp_{set}, DP_{match}}{DP_{Set}, FtDD, \varnothing, \varnothing} \quad if\ no\ other\ rule\ applies$$

$$Success\frac{\varnothing, FtDD, \varnothing, \varnothing}{FtDD} \quad if(\forall dp \in FtDD, dp.action \neq undefined)$$

$$Failure\frac{\varnothing, FtDD, \varnothing, \varnothing}{Failure} \quad if\ success\ is\ not\ applied$$

Fig. 9. Inference system for dealing with set rules

direct paths that have the action set-field, therefore in this case we will re-add the direct path dp-set to the set DP-Set and we will find all applied actions recursively. The rule Success will be applied if after updating $FtDD$ all actions are defined and the inference rule Failure will be applied otherwise.

We used two functions in this inference system:

- $modify - Field(dp - set)$: This function allows to modify fields of the direct path dp-set by replacing $field1$ by $field2$.
- $Action(DP-match)$: This function returns the action applied by direct paths in the set $Dp-match$, if all the direct paths apply the same action, otherwise, it returns **UNDEFINED**.
- $Set - action(FtDD, dp - set, act)$: This function allows to update $FtDD$ by assigning the action act to the direct path $dp - set$.

If we consider our example presented in the Sect. 1, we should find actions of different direct paths that have the action $(set - Field, Fwd(Sk))$. In our case we have one direct path:

- $dp2$ in $FtDD2$ shown in Fig. 7: By applying our inference system, we should find different direct paths in $FtDD$ that match the modified direct path $dp2$ (i.e., by replacing 172.27.1.5 by 172.27.2.7 in the field source address) and have a flow entry applied by S_3 in their field $dp.FlowEntries$. In our case we have direct path $dp2$ from $FtDD1$ and the action of this direct path is drop therefore we update our $FtDD$ by assigning the action $drop$ to the direct path $dp2$ from $FtDD2$.

We write $C \vdash_{SetField} C'$: C' is obtained from C by application of one of the inference rules of Fig. 9.

4.3 Inference System for Discovering Access-Control Misconfigurations

We have two types of misconfigurations: Total and partial misconfigurations:

- TMC: A direct path $dp_i \in FtDD$ is totally misconfigured iff it the packets mapped by this path apply a different action as applied in the security policy FC on these packets.
- PMC: A direct path $dp_i \in FtDD$ is partially misconfigured iff **some** packets mapped by this path apply a different action as applied in the security policy SP on these packets.

In Fig. 10, we propose an inference system to discover total and partial misconfigurations. Inference rules are applied on quadruple $(FtDD, TMC, PMC, dp_v)$, where $FtDD$ is the set of all flow entries decision diagrams of all paths in our network. TMC and PMC are the sets of total and partial misconfigurations respectively. dp_v is the direct path to be verified.

The inference rule parse allows to define the direct path to be verified. In most cases it is the direct path dp_i but in some cases when the dp_i.path contains a flow

$$Init \ \frac{}{FtDD, \varnothing, \varnothing, \varnothing}$$

$$Parse \ \frac{\{dp_i\} \in FtDD, TMC, PMC, \varnothing}{FtDD, TMC, PMC, dp_v} \quad where \begin{cases} dp_v = Modify - Field(dp_i) & if(dp_i.action = set - dest(f1, d2) \wedge Fwd(S_k)) \\ dp_v = dp_i & otherwise \end{cases}$$

$$Detec_{misc} \ \frac{FtDD, TMC, PMC, dp_v}{FtDD, TMC', PMC', \varnothing} \quad if(((dp_v.act \neq \text{CONTROLLER}) \vee \ !Looped(dp_v)) \wedge dom(dp_v) \nsubseteq FR^{dp_v.act})$$
$$where \begin{cases} TMC' = \{dp_v\} \cup TMC & if(dp_v.act! = undefined \wedge (dom(dp_v) \cap FR^{dp_v.act} = \varnothing)) \wedge \\ PMC' = \{dp_v\} \cup PMC & if(dp_v.act = undefined \vee (dom(dp_v) \cap FR^{dp_v.act} \neq \varnothing)) \end{cases}$$

$$Pass \ \frac{FtDD, TMC, PMC, dp_v}{FtDD, TMC', PMC', \varnothing} \quad if \ no \ other \ rule \ applies$$

$$Success \ \frac{\varnothing, \varnothing, \varnothing, \varnothing}{Success}$$

$$Failure \ \frac{\varnothing, TMC, PMC, \varnothing}{Failure} \quad if(TMC \neq \varnothing \vee PMC \neq \varnothing)$$

Fig. 10. Inference system for discovering misconfigurations

entry that have the action $set - Field$ where field is a destination address, the direct path to be verified is the direct path modified by replacing the destination address with the new one.

The main inference rule in this system is $Detect\_misc$, it deals with each direct path and compares the domain of this direct path with the set of packets of the firewall configuration that applies the same action as this direct path. If it is partially or not included by this set then we have a partial or a total misconfiguration. And if the action of the direct path is undefined then we consider this direct path partially misconfigured. The $Success$ rule is applied when we parse all direct paths of all $FtDD$ in our network without identifying a misconfiguration (total or partial). Failure is applied when at least one configuration error is identified.

For example, if we consider the network topology shown in Fig. 1 and once ensured that all direct paths have an assigned action, we proceed to the discovering of misconfigurations using our inference system. We parse all paths of $FtDD$, for each path we verify if we have an effective misconfiguration, as we explained in the previous section we have three sets of possible input addresses:

- $I1 = \{172.27.2.7, 172.27.2.3\}$ which is linked to switch S_1.
- $I2 = \{172.27.1.5\}$ which is linked to switch S_3.
- $I3 = \{*/I1UI2\}$ which is the set of possible input address sources that could income to switch S_2.

And for each $I_i \in I_{in}$, we have an $FtDD$ shown in Figs. 6, 7 and 8 respectively.

For $FtDD1$: For packets incoming from the set I_1, we have three total misconfigurations, in direct paths dp_2, dp_3 and dp_4, they apply the action $drop$, while the firewall configuration applies the action $accept$ to packets mapped by the domain of these three direct paths. We have also a partial misconfiguration, in dp_1, in fact, according to the firewall configuration shown in Fig. 2, packets that match $dp1$ and have a port number equal to 80 should be rejected, but dp_1 accepts all packets, even packets that match this port number, Therefore we should detect a PMC in this direct path.

For $FtDD2$: In this $FtDD$, There is no misconfiguration in dp_1, the action applied is $CONTROLLER$, packets will be forwarded to the firewall which is perforce with respect to the firewall. And for the direct path dp_2, there is a total misconfiguration, in fact the action assigned to the direct path dp_2 using the inference system shown in Fig. 9 is drop and the action applied by the firewall to these packets is *accept*, therefore we have one total misconfiguration in this direct path.

For $FtDD3$: For the direct path dp_1 we cannot make a decision because packet parsed by this direct path will be forwarded from S_2 to S_3 which will by his turn forward it again to S_2, therefore this direct path contains a $LOOP$ and no final decision is made. We have a TMC in dp_2, all packets matched by this direct path have a different action as applied in the firewall.

In order to prove the correctness of our approach, we start by the following definition:

- **Definition** $FtDD$ is called *misconfiguration-free* if and only if $\forall dp \in FtDD$, dp verifies these two conditions:
- (1) $dp.action \neq UNDEFINED$.
- (2) $dom(dp) \subseteq FW^{dp.action}$.
- **Theorem** if $FtDD$ is *misconfiguration-free* and $(DP_{Set}, FtDD, \emptyset, \emptyset)$ $\vdash^*_{SetField}$ *Success* then, $(FtDD, \emptyset, \emptyset, \emptyset) \vdash^*_{detectMisc}$ *Success*.
- **Proof** $FtDD$ is misconfiguration-free, then $\forall dp \in FtDD$, dp applies the same action as defined in FC, $dom(dp) \subseteq FW^{dp.action}$. It follows that at each step we apply first the inference rule $Parse$ to define the direct path to be verified dp_v, then for this direct path we try to apply the inference rule $Detect\_misc$, or $dom(dp) \subseteq FW^{dp.action}$ and $(DP_{Set}, FtDD, \emptyset, \emptyset) \vdash^*_{SetField}$ *Success* it means that $\forall dp \in FtDD$, $dp_v.action \neq undefined$, therefore, the precondition of the inference rule is not verified. It follows that in all steps $Pass$ inference rule is applied, i.e., $TMC = \emptyset$ and $PMC = \emptyset$, therefore $(FtDD, \emptyset, \emptyset, \emptyset) \vdash^*_{detectMisc}$ *Success*.

4.4   Inference System for Extracting Accepted Denied

In Fig. 11, we propose an Inference system that presents necessary and sufficient steps for extracting accepted and denied packets from a firewall configuration FR. We extract the accepted and denied packets before and after removing each rule from the firewall configuration, two cases can be faced:

- Case1: FR^{accept} (before removing r_i) is equal to FR^{accept} (after removing r_i) and FR^{deny} (before removing r_i) is equal to FR^{deny} (after removing r_i): In this case, we can remove r_i safely without altering the firewall behavior.
- Case2: FR^{accept} (before removing r_i) is different from FR^{accept} (after removing r_i) and/or FR^{deny} (before removing r_i) is different from FR^{deny} (after removing r_i): in this case we should maintain r_i in the configuration file.

Init	$\dfrac{}{(FR, \varnothing, \varnothing)}$
Add_Deny	$\dfrac{(\{r \Rightarrow deny\} \cup FR, FR^{accept}, FR^{deny})}{(FR, FR^{accept}, FR^{deny} \cup (dom(r) \smallsetminus FR^{accept}))}$
Add_Accept	$\dfrac{(\{r \Rightarrow accept\} \cup FR, FR^{accept}, FR^{deny})}{(FR, FR^{accept} \cup (dom(r) \smallsetminus FR^{deny}), FR^{deny})}$
Stop	$\dfrac{(\varnothing, FR^{accept}, FR^{deny})}{Stop}$

Fig. 11. Inference system for extracting accepted and denied packets

5 Implementation and Experimental Results

5.1 Implementation

We used all-in-one pre-built virtual machine, built by SDN Hub [5]. Wich is a Ubuntu image that has a number of SDN software and tools installed, like: SDN Controllers: OpenDaylight with support for Openflow 1.2, 1.3 and 1.4, and LINC switch. Mininet to create and run example topologies. This pre-built virtual machine contains also a JDK 1.8 and Eclipse, which allows us to easily integrate our solution.

The topology as shown in Fig. 1 is built from a Python program which uses the topology files to build the topology in the controller. The following command allows to build the configuration from the file TOPOTEST:

– $ubuntu@sdnhubvm : /mininet/examples\$ sudo$
$mn --custom\ topotest.py --topo\ toptest.$

For example to add the flow entry fe1 to the switch S1 we use the following command:

– $sh\ ovs-ofctl\ add-flow\ s1\ priority = 500, nw\_dst = 172.27.1.5, actions = 3.$

We implemented the techniques and inference systems described earlier in a software tool, using a Boolean satisfiability (SAT) based approach. This approach reduces the verification problem into Boolean formula and checks its satisfiability. In our case, in order to verify if a direct path is partially or totally misconfigured, we verify if the domain of the direct path reduced into Boolean formula is included or not in the domain of the firewall configuration reduced into two sub-domains FR^{deny} and FR^{accept} as explained in Sect. 4. So, our formalism for specifying the flow entries and the firewall configuration is a Boolean-based specification language. We have chosen also the Java developing language. On the other hand, the verification of the satisfiability of Boolean expressions is performed using Limboole [14]. This tool allows to check satisfiability respectively tautology on arbitrary structural formulas and not just satisfiability for formulas in conjunctive normal form (CNF), and can handle large set of non-quantified Boolean clauses in reasonably good time.

5.2   Complexity

For n rules in each flow table, there can be a maximum of $2n-1$ outgoing edges for a node. Therefore, the maximum number of paths in a constructed FtDD is $(2n-1)^d$, where d is the number of fields in each flow entry. After the construction of *FtDD* the discovering of misconfigurations process, explained in Sect. 4, is done on direct paths elements $dp_i.FlowEntries$ and $dp_i.action$. Therefore, for this inference system, the complexity (without counting the elementary functions) is equivalent to the complexity of operations in an ordered list and equal in this case to the complexity of parsing a list which is equal to $O(m)$ (where m is the size of a set). Thus, in our case, the complexity of this inference system is equal to $O(n^d)$, where d is the number of inspected fields. Given that d is typically small (generally we have 4 or 5 fields) our inference systems have a reasonable response time in practice. The next section confirms the above remarks.

5.3   Experimental Results

We have also conducted a set of experiments to measure the performance of our inference systems. The experiments were run on an Intel Dual core 1.6 GHz with 2 Gbyte of RAM. It is supposed that we have $IPv4$ addresses with net-masks and port numbers of 16 bit unsigned integer with range support. Figure 12 summarize our results. We consider time treatment factor that we review by varying the number of switches and flow entries. In overall terms, we consider the average processing time, in seconds, of the main procedures of FtDD construction, dealing with set Set-Field direct paths (dp_i that have action equals to $set - Field$) and *FtDD* misconfigurations detection. At the end, our tool proved a stable performance showing acceptable processing time to the treatment of complex combination of filtering flow entries.

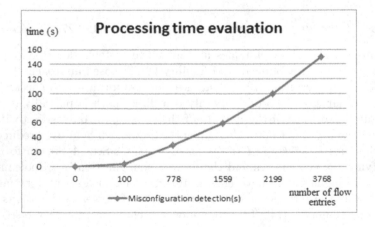

Fig. 12. Processing time evaluation

6   Conclusion

We presented in this paper a set of inference systems to automatically analyze, detect OpenFlow switches misconfigurations. More precisely, our proposal is an offline tool intended for discovering these misconfigurations by using a formal method and a data structure (FtDD), this tool can be used periodically or before updates on Flow tables occurred by the controller to verify if changes will induce further misconfigurations. The advantages of our proposal are the following: First, The detection approach is optimal, using the minimum number of operations. Second, we considered all flow entries of different switches, all paths, all actions of our switches. Third, we analyze also all modifications that can occur on packets if actions set-Field are used, which is not considered by all previous work. Fourth, we proved the correctness and completeness of our approach. While the current approach primarily focuses on discovering switches misconfigurations, in our future work, we plan to automatically resolve these misconfigurations. We are also interested in developing a tool that allows to perform automatically all proposed techniques and test this tool on Cisco Open Network Environment for Government [6] which is a comprehensive solution designed to help government network infrastructures become more open, programmable, and application-aware.

References

1. Al-Shaer, E., Al-Haj, S.: Flowchecker: configuration analysis and verification of federated openflow infrastructures. In: 3rd ACM Workshop on Assurable and Usable Security Configuration, SafeConfig 2010, Chicago, IL, USA, 4 October 2010, pp. 37–44 (2010)
2. Alimi, R., Wang, Y., Yang, Y.R.: Shadow configuration as a network management primitive. In: Proceedings of the ACM SIGCOMM 2008 Conference on Applications, Technologies, Architectures, and Protocols for Computer Communications, Seattle, WA, USA, 17–22 August 2008, pp. 111–122 (2008)
3. Ball, T.: Vericon: towards verifying controller programs in software-defined networks. In: ACM SIGPLAN Conference on Programming Language Design and Implementation, PLDI 2014, Edinburgh, United Kingdom, 09–11 June 2014, pp. 282–293 (2014)
4. Canini, M., Venzano, D., Peresíni, P., Kostic, D., Rexford, J.: A NICE way to test openflow applications. In: Proceedings of the 9th USENIX Symposium on Networked Systems Design and Implementation, NSDI 2012, San Jose, CA, USA, 25–27 April 2012, pp. 127–140 (2012)
5. All-in-one sdn app development starter vm (2018)
6. Cisco open network environment for government (2018)
7. Feamster, N., Balakrishnan, H.: Detecting BGP configuration faults with static analysis (awarded best paper). In: Proceedings of 2nd Symposium on Networked Systems Design and Implementation (NSDI 2005), Boston, Massachusetts, USA, 2–4 May 2005 (2005)
8. Foster, B., et al.: Frenetic: a network programming language. In: Proceeding of the 16th ACM SIGPLAN International Conference on Functional Programming, ICFP 2011, Tokyo, Japan, 19–21 September 2011, pp. 279–291 (2011)

9. Gouda, M.G., Liu, A.X.: Structured firewall design. Comput. Netw. **51**(4), 1106–1120 (2007)
10. Griffin, T., Wilfong, G.T.: On the correctness of IBGP configuration. In: Proceedings of the ACM SIGCOMM 2002 Conference on Applications, Technologies, Architectures, and Protocols for Computer Communication, 19–23 August 2002, Pittsburgh, PA, USA, pp. 17–29 (2002)
11. Hu, H., Han, W., Ahn, G.-J., Zhao, Z.: FLOWGUARD: building robust firewalls for software-defined networks. In: Proceedings of the Third Workshop on Hot Topics in Software Defined Networking, HotSDN 2014, Chicago, Illinois, USA, 22 August 2014, pp. 97–102 (2014)
12. Kazemian, P., Chan, M., Zeng, H., Varghese, G., McKeown, N., Whyte, S.: Real time network policy checking using header space analysis. In: NSDI, pp. 99–111. USENIX Association (2013)
13. Khurshid, A., Zou, X., Zhou, W., Caesar, M., Brighten Godfrey, P.: Veriflow: verifying network-wide invariants in real time. In: Proceedings of the 10th USENIX Symposium on Networked Systems Design and Implementation, NSDI 2013, Lombard, IL, USA, 2–5 April 2013, pp. 15–27 (2013)
14. Limboole sat solver (2018)
15. Liu, A.X., Gouda, M.G.: Diverse firewall design. IEEE Trans. Parallel Distrib. Syst. (TPDS) **19**(8), 1237–1251 (2008)
16. McKeown, N., et al.: Openflow: enabling innovation in campus networks. Comput. Commun. Rev. **38**(2), 69–74 (2008)
17. Saadaoui, A., Ben Youssef Ben Souayeh, N., Bouhoula, A.: Formal approach for managing firewall misconfigurations. In: IEEE 8th International Conference on Research Challenges in Information Science, RCIS 2014, Marrakech, Morocco, 28–30 May 2014, pp. 1–10 (2014)
18. Saâdaoui, A., Ben Youssef Ben Souayeh, N., Bouhoula, A.: FARE: fdd-based firewall anomalies resolution tool. J. Comput. Sci. **23**, 181–191 (2017)
19. Wundsam, A., Levin, D., Seetharaman, S., Feldmann, A.: Ofrewind: enabling record and replay troubleshooting for networks. In: USENIX Annual Technical Conference. USENIX Association (2011)

Energy-Efficient Computation Offloading for Multimedia Workflows in Mobile Cloud Computing

Tao Huang[1,2], Yi Chen[3], Shengjun Xue[1,3], Haojun Ji[2], Yuan Xue[3], Lianyong Qi[4(✉)], and Xiaolong Xu[3]

[1] School of Computer Science and Technology,
Silicon Lake College, Suzhou, China
nuisthuangtao@163.com
[2] Shanghai Jiading District Meteorological Bureau, Jiading, China
[3] School of Computer and Software, Nanjing University of Information Science
and Technology, Nanjing, China
[4] School of Information Science and Engineering,
Qufu Normal University, Qufu, China
lianyongqi@gmail.com

Abstract. In recent years, mobile cloud computing (MCC) is utilized to process multimedia workflows due to the limitation of battery capacity of mobile devices, which influences the experience of multimedia applications on the mobile devices. Computation offloading based on cloudlet is introduced as a novel paradigm to relieve the high latency which offloading computation to remote cloud causes. However, it is still a challenge for mobile devices to offload computation of multimedia workflows in cloudlet-based cloud computation environment to reduce energy consumption, which meets time constraints at the same time. In view of the challenge, an energy-efficient computation offloading method of multimedia workflow with multi-objective optimization is proposed in this paper. Technically, an offloading method based on cloudlet using Differential Evolution (DE) algorithm is proposed to optimize the energy consumption of the mobile devices with time constraints. Finally, massive experimental evaluations and comparison analysis validate the efficiency of our proposed method.

Keywords: Energy-efficient · Offloading · Multimedia workflow · Mobile · Cloudlet · DE

1 Introduction

The unparalleled improvements in mobile devices have changed the way that people enjoy multimedia services [1]. Audio and video documents are accessed and played easily from mobile devices. However, resource intensive multimedia applications like video encoding are in need of data processing and transmitting. Consequently, the multimedia applications drain mobile devices battery rapidly and cause high consumption of battery energy [1, 2].

© ICST Institute for Computer Sciences, Social Informatics and Telecommunications Engineering 2019
Published by Springer Nature Switzerland AG 2019. All Rights Reserved
H. Gao et al. (Eds.): TridentCom 2018, LNICST 270, pp. 113–123, 2019.
https://doi.org/10.1007/978-3-030-12971-2_7

Mobile cloud computing (MCC) could enhance the capacities of mobile devices for resource intensive multimedia applications through offloading computation to the resource-rich cloud [3, 4]. Benefit from MCC, video encoding which is extraordinarily heavy task for a mobile phone without efficient encoding applications should be off-loaded to the cloud to save much energy. However, the long distance between users and clouds could cause unpredictable delay. For the sake of reducing the latency, cloudlet is proposed as an alternative to remote clouds. Cloudlets are server clusters which are co-located with wireless Access Points (APs), and mobile users can reduce the delay by offloading latency-intensive and resource-intensive applications to local cloudlets. Comparing with the local MCC, cloudlets provide powerful computing resource closer to enhance the efficiency of cloud system [5, 6].

Whereas in reality, owing to the distributed multimedia production environment, organized multimedia workflows are desperate for maximum quality [7, 8]. For offloading multimedia workflows to remote cloud cause the high latency, offloading computation in cloudlet-based cloud computing environment is introduced to relieve the latency. With the observations above, it is still a challenge for mobile devices to offload computation of multimedia workflows in cloudlet-based cloud computation environment with a multi-objective optimization. In view of this challenge, an offloading method for multimedia workflow using Differential Evolution (DE) algorithm is proposed.

In this paper, we have made the following contributions. Firstly, we model multimedia applications by workflows, and every operation in multimedia workflows is modeled as a series of tasks in the multimedia workflow. And we analyze the average waiting time of the tasks in the cloudlet, the processing and transmission time of tasks. Then we propose an energy-efficient computation offloading method for multimedia workflow through DE algorithm to optimize the model's fitness function and constraints. Finally, the best individual is obtained through a series of mutation, crossover and selection as the solution output.

2   Problem Formulation

In this chapter, the basic concepts are proposed. Modeling multimedia applications by workflow, Optimizing multimedia workflows based on "Cloudlet", Taking the energy consumption of the mobile devices as the evaluation target. According to the priority of the multimedia workflows, the time consumption is used as a constraint.

2.1   Problem Modeling

This chapter will model the multimedia applications by workflows. Every multimedia application is modeled as a multimedia workflow, every operation in multimedia applications will be modeled as a series of tasks in the multimedia workflows, such as intelligent analysis/audit, presetting parameter template, transcoding, information extraction, content repair and encryption, etc. And the ordinal relationship between tasks will be represented by the directed graph, for example, the directed graph $G_m(V_m, \beta_m)$ represents the ordinal relationship of each task and the amount of data transferred between each task in the m-th multimedia workflow, $V_m = \{v_{1,m}, v_{2,m}, \ldots, v_{N,m}\}$ represents the set of tasks in the m-th multimedia workflow, N is the number of tasks in the m-th multimedia workflow, $\beta_m = \{r(v_{i,m}, v_{j,m}), d_{i,j} | i \neq j, 1 \leq i,j \leq N\}$ is the set of dependencies between tasks, $r(v_{i,m}, v_{j,m})$ represents $v_{i,m}$ is the predecessor task of $v_{j,m}$, $v_{j,m}$ only be executed after $v_{i,m}$ is completed, there may also be a situation where a task has more prerequisite tasks, and $d_{i,j}$ is the amount of data transferred between $v_{i,m}$ and $v_{j,m}$.

The following figure shows an example of multimedia workflow represented by the directed graph for transcoding, extracting, and encrypting video. And this multimedia workflow is mainly to transcode, extract information and encrypt the video uploaded by the mobile devices. But in reality, the different multimedia workflows may contain different operations tasks, and the execution relationships or sequence of tasks may be different (Fig. 1).

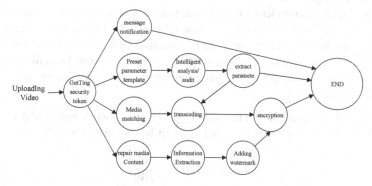

Fig. 1. An example of multimedia workflow for transcoding, extracting, and encrypting video

Usually, the tasks of multimedia workflows are executed on the mobile devices or remote cloud. However, due to the limitations of the hardware performance of the mobile devices and the high latency of the remote cloud. For the multimedia workflows that require high hardware performance and high real-time, the mobile devices and the remote cloud are not so ideal because of their own limitations. Cloudlet is widely used in the processing of multimedia workflows because it features "the higher performance than mobile devices and the lower latency than remote cloud".

Cloudlet is configured as multiple Virtual Machines (VMs) for concurrent processing the multimedia workflow, which is modeled as a 3-tuple, denoted as $CL = (N_{VM}; P_{cl}; D_{LAN})$, where N_{VM} is the number of VMs in the cloudlet, P_{cl} is the power of the cloudlet and D_{LAN} is the transmission delay in Local Area Network (LAN).

Every task in the multimedia workflows is modeled as a 2-tuple $v_{i,m} = (w_{i,m}, s_{i,m})$, where $w_{i,m}$ is the workload of task $v_{i,m}$, and $s_{i,m}$ is the offloading strategy of task $v_{i,m}$. Because the DE algorithm uses real coding, the offloading strategy is expressed as a one-dimensional real vector $S = \{s_{i,m} | i = 1, 2, \ldots, N_m; m = 1, 2, \ldots, M\}$, where $-0.5 \leq s_{i,m} < 0.5$ represents that the task $v_{i,m}$ is performed locally, $-1.5 \, d_{i,j} \, s_{i,m} < -0.5$

represents that $v_{i,m}$ is offloaded to the cloudlet and $0.5 \leq s_{i,m} < 1.5$ represents that $v_{i,m}$ is offloaded to the cloud, respectively. N_m represents the number of the tasks in the m-th multimedia workflow and M represents the number of the multimedia workflows.

2.2   Analysis of Multimedia Workflow

In this section, the model of multimedia workflows will be analyzed mainly, including: the average waiting time of the tasks in the cloudlet, the processing and transmission time of tasks, energy and time computation model, and the object function.

Average Waiting Time Analysis. Unlike the remote cloud services that have almost unlimited resources and the mobile devices that only serve the users themselves, the resource-constrained cloudlet usually need to serve multiple users around it. When the number of tasks in the task queue exceeds the number of virtual machines in the cloudlet, the subsequent tasks need to wait.

Assuming that the number of virtual machines in a cloudlet is N_{VM}, the arrival rate of tasks in the cloudlet obeys the Poisson distribution whose mean is λ, and the service time of each task in the cloudlet obeys the Exponential Distribution whose mean is μ. If the task queue in the cloudlet system is infinite length, and the tasks in the queue obey the "First In First Served" principle. According to the Queuing Theory, the "$M/M/M/\infty$" model is used.

Processing and Transmission Time Analysis. If the network bandwidth is BW, the transmission time between tasks $v_{i,m}$ and $v_{j,m}$ can be calculated as follows:

$$T_{trans}(v_{i,m}, v_{j,m}) = \frac{d_{i,j}}{BW} \tag{1}$$

The task execution time mainly includes: Waiting Time T_{wait}, Calculation Time $w_{i,m}/p$ and Network Delay D. If the offloading strategy of the task is different, the composition and calculation methods of execution time are also different. The waiting time T_{wait} is only happen when the task is executed in the cloudlet. The calculation time $w_{i,m}/p$ is related to the efficiency of the execution device, and the network delay D is related to the data transmission network (LAN or WAN). The calculation model of specific execution time is as (2). And p_l, p_{cl}, p_c represent the power of the mobile devices locally, cloudlet and cloud respectively, D_{LAN}, D_{WAN} are the transmission delay in Local Area Network (LAN) and Wide Area Network (WAN).

$$T_{exe}(v_{i,m}) = \begin{cases} \frac{w_{i,m}}{p_l}, & -0.5 \leq s_{i,m} < 0.5 \\ T_{wait} + \frac{w_{i,m}}{p_{cl}} + D_{LAN}, & -1.5 \leq s_{i,m} < -0.5 \\ \frac{w_{i,m}}{p_c} + D_{WAN}, & 0.5 \leq s_{i,m} < 1.5 \end{cases} \tag{2}$$

2.3   Energy and Time Computation Model

The energy consumption of data transmission between $v_{i,m}$ and $v_{j,m}$ is:

$$E_{trans}(v_{i,m}, v_{j,m}) = \frac{d_{i,j}}{BW} * p_{\mathrm{t}} \tag{3}$$

p_t is the power of mobile devices during data transmission;

When the task is executed on the mobile devices, the mobile devices are active at this time and the power p is p_a. On the contrary, when the task is executed in the cloudlet or the cloud, the mobile devices are idle and the power p is p_i. So the power consumption of $v_{i,m}$ is

$$E_{\mathrm{exe}}(v_{i,m}) = T_{\mathrm{exe}}(v_{i,m}) * p \tag{4}$$

Then, the total energy consumption of the mobile devices is calculated as follows:

$$E_{app,m}(S) = \sum_{v_{i,m} \in V} E_{exe}(v_{i,m}) + \sum_{r(v_{i,m}, v_{j,m}) \subseteq \beta} E_{trans}(v_{i,m}, v_{j,m}),$$
$$m \in \{1, 2, \ldots, M\}. \tag{5}$$

2.4   Object Function

The total energy consumption of the mobile devices is used as the evaluation target, and the deadline of each multimedia workflow is used as a constraint. Due to each multimedia workflow has a different priority. The scaling factor F_{PR} is used to scale or expand the execution time of the multimedia workflows.

3   An Energy-Efficient Computation Offloading Method for Multimedia Workflow Using DE Algorithm

This chapter mainly encodes the energy-efficient computation offloading model of multimedia workflows, and optimizes the model's fitness function and constraint using the DE Algorithm, the non-dominated sorting approach and the crowded-comparison are used in the optimization process. Through a series operations of mutation, crossover and selection, the best individual is finally obtained as the optimal solution output. Below we will give a detailed optimization process:

Algorithm 1. Calculate the completion time for the multimedia workflow
Input: m-th multimedia workflow, offloading strategy S
Output: Completion time of the multimedia workflow $T_{app,m}(S)$
1: $pre_v=\emptyset, D^*=\emptyset, T_{app,m}(S)=0$
2: if $v_{j,m}$ is the first node in $G_m(V, \beta)$ then
3:    $D(v_{j,m})=T_{exe}(v_{j,m})$
4: else
5:    add $v_{j,m}$ to pre_v
6: end if
7: for $v_{j,m} \in pre_v$ do
8:    $D(v_{j,m})= D(v_{i,m})+T_{trans}(v_{i,m}, v_{j,m})+T_{exe}(v_{j,m})$
9:    add $D(v_{j,m})$ to D^*
10: end for
11: for $d \in D^*$ do
12:    if $T_{app,m}(S)<d$ then
13:        $T_{app,m}(S)=d$
14:    end if
15: end for
16: return $T_{app,m}(S)$

3.1 Encoding

DE algorithm using real-coded, so each task of multimedia workflows has an integer index organized from 0 and a real value representing an offloading strategy of the task. The offloading strategies of all tasks in the multimedia workflows are combined into an individual. Each individual represents an implementation of multimedia workflows and a population consists of multiple individuals. The DE algorithm performs evolutionary operations on each generation of population to seek the optimal execution strategy for the optimization problem.

3.2 Fitness Function and Constraint

In this paper, the DE algorithm uses the energy consumption of the mobile devices as the fitness function to find the offloading strategies that can make the total energy consumption the lowest. Each deadline of multimedia workflows is a constraint, so that each multimedia workflow must be completed within the deadline, Algorithm 1 explains how to calculate the completion time of multimedia workflow. Then DE algorithm performs evolutionary operations on every generation of population to find the optimal execution strategy for multimedia workflows.

3.3 Optimize the Multimedia Workflows Using DE Algorithm

Initialization. The size of individual N is determined by the number of tasks in all multimedia workflows. Each value of gene in the individual represents the offloading strategies of the tasks corresponding to the index. The offloading strategy values range from $[-1.5, 1.5)$, and its meaning has already been introduced in the Basic Concepts section. Then the experiment needs to determine the parameters of the DE algorithm, such as the appropriate number of evolutionary iterations G and the population size $2NP$. Finally, the experiment also needs to determine the appropriate crossover Probability CR, the mutation probability F and mutation strategy.

The first-generation populations P_1 is generated by randomly assigning values for each gene of each individual in the range $[-1.5, 1.5)$.

Evolution. Combining the multiple evaluation target, The "Pareto sorting" is used for the population to obtain a set L with multiple layers of dominating solutions, and calculate the "crowd distance" for each layer of dominating solutions. From the first layer of dominating solution, the preferred individuals are selected to fill in R_{g+1} until the population size of R_{g+1} is NP. Then DE algorithms performs evolutionary operations on the population R_{g+1}, including mutations, crossovers, and selections to generate a new populations O_{g+1} whose size is also NP. Finally, R_{g+1} and O_{g+1} are combined into the next-generation populations P_{g+1}, and the optimization continues. Until the termination condition is satisfied, the optimal offloading strategies and the energy consumption for all mobile devices are output.

4   Comparison and Analysis of Experimental Results

This chapter mainly uses four kinds of offloading methods: Benchmark, CBO, CLBO and DECO. Among them, Benchmark, CBO and CLBO represent that all tasks of multimedia workflows will be executed in mobile devices, remote cloud and cloudlet respectively. DECO assigns the tasks of multimedia workflows to the mobile devices, remote cloud, and cloudlet for execution using the DE algorithm intelligently, to optimize the energy consumption of the mobile devices.

4.1   Experimental Settings

In this experiment, the performance of the method was tested by optimizing different numbers of multimedia workflows. Each multimedia workflow contains 13 tasks, and the workload for tasks in every multimedia workflow are set to {0; 20; 50; 8; 20; 30; 80; 60; 30; 50; 20; 40; 0}. But the ordinal relationship of each task and the amount of data transferred between each task in the different multimedia workflow are different. In this experiment, the parameter settings are as follows: the power of mobile devices when the CPU is idle and active are 0.001 W and 0.5 W, respectively, and the transmission power of mobile devices is 0.1 W. The processing capacity of mobile devices, cloudlet and cloud are 500 MHz, 2000 MHz and 3000 MHz, respectively. The delay of LAN and WAN are 1 ms and 30 ms, respectively. The LANs and WANs bandwidth are 100 kb/s and 50 kb/s. The average waiting time of tasks in the cloudlet is 20 ms. And the experimental datasets can be accessed in the following link: https://drive.google.com/open?id=1nc-QVdthUCjUSzazDgYxMIh0EGEN-r_L.

4.2 Performance Evaluation

In this section, three groups of experiments were conducted by selecting 3, 4 and 5 multimedia workflows: Figs. 2 and 3 show the comparison of energy consumption and completion time of mobile devices and Fig. 4 shows the assignment of all tasks for multimedia workflows using four kinds of offloading methods in three groups of experiments.

It can be clearly seen from Figs. 2 and 3 that in the three groups of experiments, energy consumption and completion time using the Benchmark offloading method are much higher than the other three methods. Because the computing performance of the mobile devices is so limited compared to remote cloud and cloudlet that it will certainly consume a lot of energy and computing time. However, when the tasks of multimedia workflows are offloaded to the remote cloud or the cloudlet, the mobile devices only needs to transmit data and wait for results instead of performing calculation tasks that consume a lot of energy and time.

Secondly, Figs. 2 and 3 also show that CLBO is better than CBO because CLBO has lower network latency than CBO.

But this does not mean that the performance of CLBO will always be better than CBO, because CBO has higher computational performance than CLBO. and when there are too many tasks in the cloudlet, the tasks will have waiting time. They have their own advantages and disadvantages. However, there is no doubt that the effect of DECO must be better than the other three methods. This can also be clearly seen from the experimental results. Because during the optimization of multimedia workflows using the DE algorithm, the other three offloading methods are just the special states of DECO. For example, the strategy of CLBO and CBO is to take the value of each gene of every individual in the population between [−1.5, −0.5) and [0.5, 1.5) respectively.

The three groups of experimental results in Fig. 4 show that in this experiment, the effect of DECO was better than the other three offloading methods. It is precisely because of the optimization of multimedia workflows using the DE algorithm that the tasks of multimedia workflows are reasonably allocated to the corresponding devices (mobile devices, cloudlet, and remote cloud).

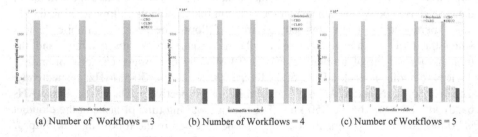

(a) Number of Workflows = 3   (b) Number of Workflows = 4   (c) Number of Workflows = 5

Fig. 2. The comparison of energy consumption

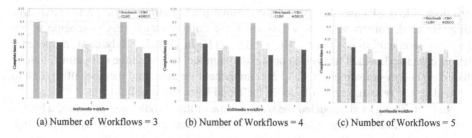

(a) Number of Workflows = 3   (b) Number of Workflows = 4   (c) Number of Workflows = 5

Fig. 3. The completion time

(a) Number of tasks = 39   (b) Number of tasks = 52   (c) Number of tasks = 65

Fig. 4. The assignment of all tasks for multimedia workflow

At the same time, through the results of this group of experiments, it can be seen that the reason that the effect of DECO is closer to CLBO is that most of the tasks in multimedia workflows are still assigned to execute in the cloudlet.

Finally, it can be confirmed that the DECO is definitely the best one among the 4 offloading methods. And this has been verified in this experiment. However, due to the limitation of the scale of this experimental data set, the respective advantages of the remote cloud and the cloud cannot be fully reflected. In practical applications, the scale and complexity of multimedia workflows running in remote cloud and cloudlet are far greater than the data sets of this experiment. At that time, the optimization effect of multimedia workflows using DECO will be even more obvious.

5 Related Work

In recent years, with the development of multimedia applications on mobile devices, MCC which has faster data processing rate is beneficial to process data from multimedia applications [9–12]. Additionally, offloading multimedia workflows which have complex functionality to the cloudlets to save energy and processing time of multimedia applications [13, 14].

Deng et al. proposed and optimized a computation computing strategy for workflows which are related to mobile devices. Liu et al. proposed a hybrid model which transferring data through multiple wireless networks, and formulated the offloading problem in hybrid wireless networks in [10]. In [14], Shah-Mansouri et al. developed a dynamic task scheduler which could decide the offloading strategy on the cloud service provider side (CSP) and determined the optimal pricing strategy via profit maximization. He et al. constructed a new privacy-aware authentication (PAA) scheme which has less computation costs for MCC services [11]. In [13], Elgendy et al. proposed a novel framework which utilizes an optimization model to decide the offloading strategy based on energy consumption, CPU use, implementing time, and memory utilization to offload intensive computation tasks to the cloud from the mobile device.

In [10], Zhang et al. modeled the waiting time of the cloudlet and proposed a hybrid computing offloading algorithm which minimizes the all energy consumption that mobile devices cause. Besides, Rimal et al. presented a novel cloudlet-aware resource management scheme to reduce the offload delay [12].

To the best of our knowledge, there are few researches on the multimedia workflows scheduling through offloading multimedia workflows to the cloudlets with multiobjective optimization. With the observations above, it is still a challenge to realize an efficient multimedia workflow offloading method which reduces the energy consumption and meets the time constraint. In view of this challenge, an offloading method for multimedia workflow using DE algorithm is proposed.

6 Conclusion and Future Work

The existing multimedia workflow offloading methods barely take both time and energy consumption into account. In this paper, an energy-efficient computation offloading method of multimedia workflow based on cloudlet is proposed. We analyze execution time and construct a model of energy and time computation of mobile device. The method based on cloudlet using DE algorithm is designed to optimize the energy consumption of the mobile devices within deadline. Through ample experimental evaluation, validate the efficiency of our proposed method is proved.

Based on the work done in this paper, we will adjust and extend our multimedia workflow offloading method to reduce the energy and time consumption of multimedia applications. We will implement the offloading method to improve the experience of users when uploading videos, and keep updating our method according to the real-life performance.

Acknowledgement. This research is supported by the Research Project of Shanghai Meteorological Bureau Scientific under Grant No. TD201807 and the National Science Foundation of China under grant no. 61702277, no. 61672276, no. 61772283, no. 61402167 and no. 61672290, the Key Research and Development Project of Jiangsu Province under Grant No. BE2015154 and BE2016120, and Natural Science Foundation of Jiangsu Province (Grant No. BK20171458). Besides, this work is also supported by The Startup Foundation for Introducing Talent of NUIST, the open project from State Key Laboratory for Novel Software Technology.

References

1. Kaewmahingsa, K., Bhattarakosol, P.: Mobile cloud system: a solution for multimedia retrieval via mobile phones. In: International Conference on Computing & Convergence Technology, vol. 8652, no. 5, pp. 36–40 (2012)
2. Altamimi, M., Palit, R., Naik, K., Nayak, A.: Energy-as-a-Service (EaaS): on the efficacy of multimedia cloud computing to save smartphone energy. In: IEEE Fifth International Conference on Cloud Computing, pp. 764–771 (2012)
3. Chen, X.: Decentralized computation offloading game for mobile cloud computing. IEEE Trans. Parallel Distrib. Syst. **26**(4), 974–983 (2015)
4. Kovachev, D., Yu, T., Klamma, R.: Adaptive computation offloading from mobile devices into the cloud. In: IEEE International Symposium on Parallel & Distributed Processing with Applications, pp. 784–791 (2012)
5. Liu, Y., Lee, M.: Adaptive multi-resource allocation for cloudlet-based mobile cloud computing system. IEEE Trans. Mob. Comput. **15**(10), 2398–2410 (2016)
6. Xu, Z., Liang, W., Xu, W., et al.: Efficient algorithms for capacitated cloudlet placements. IEEE Trans. Parallel Distrib. Syst. **27**(10), 2866–2880 (2016)
7. Hazekamp, N., Kremer-Herman, N., Tovar, B., Meng, H., Choudhury, O.: Combining static and dynamic storage management for data intensive scientific workflows. IEEE Trans. Parallel Distrib. Syst. **29**(2), 338–350 (2018)
8. Liu, P., Wang, R., Ding, J., Yin, X.: Performance modeling and evaluating workflow of ITS: real-time positioning and route planning (1), 1–15 (2017)
9. Deng, S., Huang, L., Taheri, J., Zomaya, A.Y.: Computation offloading for service workflow in mobile cloud computing. IEEE Trans. Parallel Distrib. Syst. **26**(12), 3317–3329 (2015)
10. Zhang, J., et al.: Hybrid Computation offloading for smart home automation in mobile cloud computing. Pers. Ubiquit. Comput. **22**(1), 121–134 (2018)
11. He, D., Kumar, N., Khan, M.K., et al.: Efficient privacy-aware authentication scheme for mobile cloud computing services. IEEE Syst. J. **12**(2), 1621–1631 (2018)
12. Li, R., Shen, C., He, H., Xu, Z., Xu, C.Z.: A lightweight secure data sharing scheme for mobile cloud computing. IEEE Trans. Cloud Comput. **6**(2), 344–357 (2018)
13. Elgendy, I., Zhang, W., Liu, C., Hsu, C.: An efficient and secured framework for mobile cloud computing. IEEE Trans. Cloud Comput. (2018)
14. Xue, S., Peng, Y., Xu, X., Zhang, J., Shen, C., Ruan, F.: DSM: a dynamic scheduling method for concurrent workflows in cloud environment. Cluster Comput. **3**, 1–14 (2017)

A Secure Contained Testbed
for Analyzing IoT Botnets

Ayush Kumar$^{(\boxtimes)}$ and Teng Joon Lim

Department of Electrical and Computer Engineering,
National University of Singapore, Singapore 119077, Singapore
ayush.kumar@u.nus.edu, eleltj@nus.edu.sg

Abstract. Many security issues have come to the fore with the increasingly widespread adoption of Internet-of-Things (IoT) devices. The Mirai attack on Dyn DNS service, in which vulnerable IoT devices such as IP cameras, DVRs and routers were infected and used to propagate large-scale DDoS attacks, is one of the more prominent recent examples. IoT botnets, consisting of hundreds-of-thousands of bots, are currently present "in-the-wild" at least and are only expected to grow in the future, with the potential to cause significant network downtimes and financial losses to network companies. We propose, therefore, to build testbeds for evaluating IoT botnets and design suitable mitigation techniques against them. A DETERlab-based IoT botnet testbed is presented in this work. The testbed is built in a secure contained environment and includes ancillary services such as DHCP, DNS as well as botnet infrastructure including CnC and scanListen/loading servers. Developing an IoT botnet testbed presented us with some unique challenges which are different from those encountered in non-IoT botnet testbeds and we highlight them in this paper. Further, we point out the important features of our testbed and illustrate some of its capabilities through experimental results.

Keywords: Internet of Things · IoT · Malware · Mirai · Botnet ·
Testbed

1 Introduction

The Internet of things (IoT) [1] refers to the network of low-power, limited processing capability sensing devices which can send/receive data to/from other devices using wireless technologies such as RFID (Radio Frequency Identification), Zigbee, WiFi, Bluetooth, cellular etc. IoT devices are being deployed in a number of applications such as wearables, home automation, smart grids, environmental monitoring, infrastructure management, industrial automation, agricultural automation, healthcare and smart cities. Some of the popular platforms for IoT are Samsung SmartThings (consumer IoT for device management) and Amazon Web Services IoT, Microsoft Azure IoT, Google Cloud Platform

© ICST Institute for Computer Sciences, Social Informatics and Telecommunications Engineering 2019
Published by Springer Nature Switzerland AG 2019. All Rights Reserved
H. Gao et al. (Eds.): TridentCom 2018, LNICST 270, pp. 124–137, 2019.
https://doi.org/10.1007/978-3-030-12971-2_8

(enterprise IoT for cloud storage and data analytics). The number of IoT devices deployed globally by 2020 is expected to be in the range of 20–30 billion [2]. The number of devices has been increasing steadily (albeit at a slower rate than some earlier generous predictions), and this trend is expected to hold in the future.

IoT devices are being increasingly targeted by hackers using malware (malicious software) as they are easier to infect than conventional computers for the following reasons [3–5]:

– There are many legacy IoT devices connected to the Internet with no security updates.
– Security is given a low priority within the development cycle of IoT devices.
– Implementing conventional cryptography in IoT devices is computationally expensive due to processing power and memory constraints.
– Many IoT devices have weak login credentials either provided by the manufacturer or configured by users.
– IoT device manufacturers sometimes leave *backdoors* (such as an open port) to provide support for the device remotely.
– Often, consumer IoT devices are connected to the Internet without going through a firewall.

In a widely publicized attack, the IoT malware *Mirai* was used to propagate the biggest DDoS (Distributed Denial-of-Service) attack on record on October 21, 2016. The attack targeted the Dyn DNS (Domain Name Service) servers [6] and generated an attack throughput of the order of 1.2 Tbps. It disabled major internet services such as Amazon, Twitter and Netflix. The attackers had infected IoT devices such as IP cameras and DVR recorders with Mirai, thereby creating an army of bots (botnet) to take part in the DDoS attack. Apart from Mirai, there are other IoT malware which operate using a similar brute force technique of scanning random IP addresses for open ports and attempting to login using a built-in dictionary of commonly used credentials. BASHLITE [7], Remaiten [8], and Hajime [9] are some examples of these IoT malware.

Bots compromised by Mirai or similar IoT malware can be used for DDoS attacks, phishing and spamming [10]. These attacks can cause network downtime for long periods which may lead to financial loss to network companies, and leak users' confidential data. McAfee reported in April 2017 [11] that about 2.5 million IoT devices were infected by Mirai in late 2016. Bitdefender mentioned in its blog in September 2017 [12] that researchers had estimated at least 100,000 devices infected by Mirai or similar malware revealed daily through telnet scanning telemetry data. Further, many of the infected devices are expected to remain infected for a long time. Therefore, there is a substantial motivation for studying these IoT botnets so as to characterize, detect and develop effective countermeasures against them.

A comprehensive IoT botnet testbed environment will be quite useful for researchers working towards this goal. Further, the testbed can be used to generate useful ground truth data for researchers to evaluate the effectiveness of their proposed IoT botnet detection algorithms. As pointed out in [13], botnet emulation studies in controlled laboratory environments have a number of advantages (e.g. closeness to real-world botnets, greater degree of safety and control over experiment environment, fewer legal and ethical issues) when it comes to botnet research compared to analytical modelling, simulation studies, botnet binary reverse engineering and in-the-wild botnet analysis.

In this work, we present a testbed environment built using the National Cybersecurity R&D Lab (NCL) [14] infrastructure and consisting of physical and virtual machines (VMs) which can be used to study Mirai-like IoT botnets. As pointed out later, the same testbed can be modified to work with other IoT botnets as well. The testbed includes ancillary services such as Domain Name Service (DNS), Dynamic Host Configuration Protocol (DHCP), botnet infrastructure which includes Command-and-Control (CnC) and scanListen/loading servers, and a secure contained environment for testing. The last two services are provided by DETERLab [15], which provides the software stack on which the NCL testbed is based. A secure contained environment is especially critical since many of the botnets are capable of further infecting devices connected to the Internet. This testbed is mainly targeted at cyber security researchers who can easily and quickly bootstrap IoT botnet experiments on our testbed. To the best of our knowledge, this is the first testbed to emulate the full behavior of an IoT botnet. In the subsequent sections, we review published research on botnet testbeds. We also elaborate on our experience setting up the various components of the testbed and the related challenges that we faced. Finally, we include some experimental results from our testbed that illustrate its capabilities.

2   Related Work

There have been several research works on the study of botnets through testbeds. Barford et al. [16] have presented a toolkit for Emulab-enabled testbeds (such as DETERlab) called Botnet Evaluation Environment (BEE), designed to provide bots and botnets for experimentation in a scalable and secure/self-contained environment. BEE includes a library of OS/bot images to be run on physical and virtual machines as well as a set of services and tools required for botnet evaluation such as DHCP, DNS, IRC, VM monitors and honeypots. [17] has proposed a composable botnet framework called SLINGbot which can be used to construct botnets with different (Command and Control) C2 structures (including potential future botnet C2 structures), simulate botnet traffic, characterize it and develop botnet defense techniques.

In [13], the authors have argued for isolated in-the-lab at-scale botnet experimentation and evaluated an emulated 3000-node Waledac botnet. Further, they have also validated a defense technique (using sybil attack) against the botnet. [18] has argued for large-scale botnet emulation that is at par with actual botnets (hundreds of thousands to millions of bots) and potentially discover issues that show up at that scale. The authors have presented a prototype testbed with 600,000 Linux VMs or 62,000 Windows 7 VMs on a 520 node computing cluster through over-budgeting of processor and memory resources and other techniques. Since few works have paid attention to containment in botnet emulation, a malware execution farm, *GQ* has been presented in [19] which focuses on methodical development of explicit containment policies for malware measurement and analysis.

ElSheikh et al. [20] have addressed the lack of publicly available botnet research datasets by creating an in-lab botnet experimentation testbed in a contained environment and using it to generate botnet datasets. [21] has implemented an HTTP (Hypertext Transfer Protocol)-based botnet testbed for performing HTTP GET flooding attacks against web servers. The authors have also provided real-time data sets (including http bot traces) for researchers to evaluate such botnets and proposed countermeasures against DDoS attacks from those botnets. Finally, in [22], the authors have presented a controlled network environment based on VMware virtualization technology, called V-Network, for analyzing network worm propagation patterns and evaluating countermeasure systems.

This paper makes an important contribution since there has been no work till now on creating IoT botnet testbeds emulating the full behavior of IoT malware. Our testbed is similar to [16] in the sense that it is also based on DETERlab and provides services such as DNS, DHCP, CnC etc. but the challenges encountered by us (as pointed out in Sect. 3.3) were different because the testbed in [16] was focused on PC-based bots and not IoT bots. In comparison to [13] and [18], our current focus is not on scalability since we can increase the number of bots in our testbed easily by installing more VMs per physical machine and adding more physical machines. However, we intend to look into their techniques in the future to increase the number of bots in our testbed to more accurately represent real-world IoT botnets. We are in the process of collecting datasets for the IoT botnet research community, similar to [20], and hope to release them in near future. Out testbed is not restricted to specific attacks such as HTTP flooding [21] and we also use virtualization to create multiple bots on a physical machine, albeit not through VMWare hypervisor as done in [22].

3 IoT Botnet Testbed

In this section, we begin by giving an overview of the operation of Mirai, followed by a detailed discussion on the process of setting up various components of our IoT botnet testbed. We move on to highlight the challenges during testbed setup and how they were overcome. Finally, the major features of our testbed are pointed out.

3.1 Overview of Mirai

The Mirai [23] setup consists of three major components: *bot, scanListen/loading* server, and the *CnC* (Command-and-Control) server. The *CnC* server also functions as a MySQL [24] database server. User accounts can be created in this database for customers who wish to hire DDoS-as-a-service. The database on CnC server consists of three tables: history, user and whitelist. They are assigned bots and can use them to launch a DDoS attack against their target services. There are a number of attack options available in Mirai: UDP flood, SYN flood,

ACK flood, TCP stomp flood, UDP plain flood, Valve source engine specific flood, DNS resolver flood, GRE IP flood, GRE Ethernet flood and HTTP flood.

The operation of Mirai is illustrated in Fig. 1. Once an IoT device is infected with Mirai (and becomes a bot), it first attempts to connect to the listening *CnC* server by resolving its domain name and opening a socket connection. Thereafter, it starts scanning the network by sending SYN packets to random IP addresses and waiting for them to respond. This process may take a long time since the bot has to go through a large number of IP addresses. Once it finds a vulnerable device with a TELNET port open, it attempts to open a socket connection to that device and emulates the TELNET protocol. Then it attempts to login using a list of default credentials and if successful, it reports the IP address of the discovered device and the working TELNET login credentials to the listening *scanListen* server. The *scanListen* server sends that information to the *loader* which again logs in to the discovered device using the details received from the *scanListen* server. Once logged in, the *loader* downloads the Mirai bot binary to that device and the new bot connects to the *CnC* server and starts scanning the network.

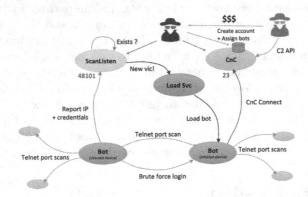

Fig. 1. Operation of various components of Mirai *(Source: Radware [25])*

3.2   Installing Testbed Components

The testbed shown in Fig. 2 was configured on a computing cluster isolated from the Internet. Each cluster node has two Intel Xeon E5-2620 processors, 64 GB DDR4 ECC memory and runs Ubuntu 14.04 LTS standard image. The first step was to configure a local authoritative DNS server on one of the testbed nodes because infected Mirai bots connect to CnC and scanListen servers using domain names instead of fixed IP addresses. The reason behind this design can be that the malware authors did not want the CnC/scanListen servers to be taken down if their IP addresses were identified by security personnel. If domain names are used for connection instead, the IP addresses mapped to those domain names can be easily changed if they have been identified and blocked. Originally, the Mirai source code (*bot/resolv.c*) uses the Google DNS servers located at IP

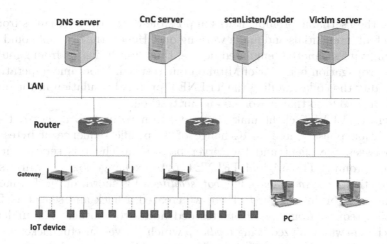

Fig. 2. Testbed used to simulate Mirai behavior

address *8.8.8.8* for domain name-to-IP address conversion. However, since we were working on a secure isolated testbed with no outside Internet connectivity, we could not use Google DNS servers. Therefore, it became essential for us to configure a local DNS server on our testbed. We used BIND9 (Berkeley Internet Naming Daemon) to configure a local name server as a primary master, creating forward and reverse zone files. The next step entailed configuring a CnC server (by creating a MYSQL database) on a testbed node and the scanListen/loader on another node.

The IoT devices used in our testbed are Raspberry Pi (RPi) devices emulated using QEMU [26], an open source machine emulator and hardware virtualizer. Each RPi device runs Raspbian (Wheezy version) and is configured with ARM 1176 (v6) CPU and 256 MB of RAM. The CnC and scanListen server domain names and port numbers were updated in *bot/table.c* file in the RPi. Since the emulated RPi devices need to connect to the CnC and scanListen servers using their domain names, the details of local DNS server were added to the */etc/resolv.conf* files in emulated devices which query the local DNS server to get the IP addresses corresponding to the domain names and then connect to those IP addresses. The codes for bot, CnC server, scanListen server and loader were compiled using the script, *mirai/build.sh.* Since we wanted to compile the bot binaries for RPi (which runs on ARM platform) on a testbed node running on x86 platform, we also had to setup cross-compilers using the *scripts/cross-compile.sh* script.

3.3 Challenges Encountered in Testbed Setup

One of the major challenges was the TELNET protocol emulation in Mirai source code. When the original bot binary compiled from source code was run on an emulated RPi device, it was unable to receive the TELNET username prompt.

Without the username prompt, it was impossible to try the usernames from the list of default credentials and find a working one. Hence, the first bot could never successfully infect another emulated device, thus preventing us from simulating the real propagation behavior of Mirai on our testbed. It became imperative for us to modify the code handling the TELNET protocol emulation in the original Mirai source code so that it worked on our testbed.

When a TELNET client makes a connection request to a server, there is a negotiation phase where an exchange of a specific sequence of bytes takes place between the client and the server before the client is served with the username prompt. The original TELNET byte exchange logic in Mirai source code (function: *consume_iacs()*, file: *bot/scanner.c*) is shown in Fig. 5. Since this logic was not working on our testbed, we created a hack and sent a TELNET connection request from one of our testbed nodes to another. The underlying byte exchange was analyzed using *tcpdump* which is a very useful packet analyzer that is usually installed by default on Linux machines. We modified the code in *consume_iacs()* function to replicate the above byte exchange sequence which is depicted in Fig. 3. Again, after the username prompt is served to the client and the username is entered, there is a byte exchange between the TELNET client and server before the password prompt is served. Therefore, we modified the code in *consume_pass_prompt()* with the required byte sequence so that the testbed bot is served the password prompt, as shown in Fig. 4.

Fig. 3. Changes made in *consume_iacs()* function in Mirai source code

For the emulated RPi (on which Mirai binary is executed) to scan nearby devices, it needs to connect to the host network. By default, QEMU assigns a static IP address (10.0.2.15) to the emulated RPi if the user has not specified any network interfaces in the script that brings up the RPi, thereby leaving no connectivity between RPi and host. One of the ways to achieve this connectivity is by using bridge-TAP configuration. A network bridge refers to a device that connects two separate network segments using the same communication protocol, allowing them to operate as a single aggregate network. TAP interface is a virtual network interface that sends and receives layer 2 packets such as Ethernet frames not through a physical "wire", but instead by writing and reading data respectively from user-space programs. We used *brctl* to configure Ethernet bridge on the host, *tunctl* to create and manage TAP interfaces and *libvrt* virtualization management library to automatically setup a DHCP server and bridge (*virbr0*) on the host. The *virbr0* comes up with a default IP address(192.168.122.1), so the IP address had to be changed for each host using *virsh* utility. The TAP interface was bound to the bridge and the QEMU RPi was brought up with a network interface attached to the TAP device. Any packets sent from the RPi are now written to the TAP interface and forwarded by the attached bridge to the host network. Similarly, packets sent from the host network are forwarded through the bridge to the attached TAP interface from where they are read by RPi operating system. Since we were emulating multiple QEMU VMs on a physical node, a base Raspbian image was created in *qcow2* format and using it as a backing file, we generated disk images which store only the differences from base image to avoid using multiple raw image files and save on storage space.

```
static int consume_pass_prompt(struct scanner_connection *conn)
{
    char *pch;
    int i, prompt_ending = -1;

    uint8_t *ptr = conn->rdbuf;

    char tmp1[] = {0xff, 0xfa, 0x1f, 0x00, 0xcc, 0x00, 0x33, 0xff, 0xf0};
    char tmp2[] = {0xff, 0xfa, 0x1f, 0x00, 0xcc, 0x00, 0x34, 0xff, 0xf0};

    sleep(2);
    send(conn->fd, &tmp1[0], 9, MSG_NOSIGNAL);
    sleep(2);
    send(conn->fd, &tmp2[0], 9, MSG_NOSIGNAL);
    sleep(2);

    ptr += conn->rdbuf_pos;

    for (i = conn->rdbuf_pos - 1; i > 0; i--)
    {
        if (conn->rdbuf[i] == ':' || conn->rdbuf[i] == '>' || conn->rdbuf[i] == '$' || conn->rdbuf[i] == '#')
        {
            prompt_ending = i + 1;
            break;
        }
    }

    if (prompt_ending == -1)
    {
        int tmp;

        if ((tmp = util_memsearch(conn->rdbuf, conn->rdbuf_pos, "assword", 7)) != -1)
            prompt_ending = tmp;
    }

    if (prompt_ending == -1)
        return 0;
    else
        return prompt_ending;
}
```

Fig. 4. Changes made in *consume_pass_prompt()* function in Mirai source code

3.4   Testbed Features

The main features of our IoT botnet testbed are listed below:

– Using Network Simulator (NS) scripts, users can conveniently start, stop, modify and restart malware experiments instead of employing manual configuration.

- The emulated Raspberry Pi devices are quite close to the real-world IoT devices in terms of the platform, operating system, applications and networking capabilities.
- Our testbed can be scaled to add more IoT devices (by increasing the number of QEMU VMs per physical machine), gateways, routers and other network devices as per user simulation requirements. It also supports the integration of both physical and virtual devices.
- The testbed topology, i.e. the way the routers, gateways and IoT devices are connected to each other, can be changed to simulate different types of networks.
- More advanced versions or derivatives of Mirai malware can be tested on our testbed since the ancillary infrastructure required (consisting of DNS server, CnC server, scanListen/loader) is already configured. The only remaining requirement is to run the specific malware binary on the emulated IoT devices.
- IoT malware exploiting software vulnerabilities (such as Reaper, Satori etc.) can also be tested on our testbed by running the corresponding bot binaries/compiled source codes/exploit codes on the emulated RPi devices and making a few other modifications in the ancillary services and botnet infrastructure.

4   Experimental Results

As shown in Fig. 2, the local DNS server, CnC (Command-and-Control) server, scanListen/loading server and the victim server (which is to be attacked through DDoS) are all connected to a single LAN. In practice, all the above servers are parts of different sub-networks connected to the Internet. The NCL testbed has a limitation of maximum two network interfaces per physical node, thereby restricting us from simulating more realistic networks with multiple connections. However, this restriction does not impair our testbed functions such as scanning of vulnerable devices, bot-CnC communications, infection of emulated devices and attacks launched from infected devices. These functions are not dependent on the relative placement of DNS server, CnC server, scanListen/loading server and victim server in the network. Further connected to the same LAN are three routers, two of which are connected to IoT gateways (physical devices acting as a bridge between IoT devices and the cloud) and the third one is connected to non-IoT devices (e.g. PC). Finally, each gateway is connected to 10 IoT devices. We chose this gateway-IoT device topology since it is used in a number of IoT deployments (such as IP cameras, smart lighting devices, wearables etc.). The IoT devices can run a video streaming server to simulate the operation of an IP camera (IoT device used in Mirai attack on Dyn). A few IoT devices were configured to have their TELNET port number 23 open and listening for connections.

We have plotted the volume of bot-CnC traffic with time for a single bot (traffic volume in packets per second) in Fig. 6. As expected, there are busy

IF first byte != 255, break;

IF first two bytes = [255 255], continue;

IF first two bytes = [255 253], send [255 251 31] AND send [255, 250, 31, 0, 80, 0, 24, 255, 240];

IF first two bytes = [255 253] AND third byte != 31,

     FOR first three bytes, (IF byte = 253, change to 252) AND (IF byte = 251, change to 253)

     Send all bytes in buffer;

IF first byte = 255 AND second byte != 253,

     FOR first three bytes, (IF byte = 253 change to 252) AND (IF byte = 251 change to 253)

     Send all bytes in buffer;

Fig. 5. TELNET client-server negotiation logic used in Mirai source code

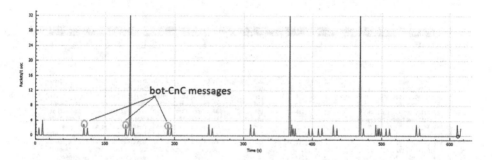

Fig. 6. Volume of bot-CnC traffic with time

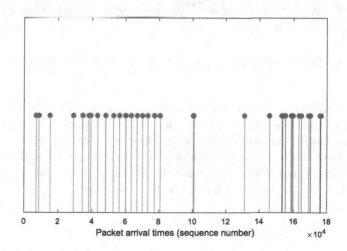

Fig. 7. Transmission times of bot scanning packets

and non-busy periods in the bot-CnC traffic. The busy period is when there is exchange of keep-alive messages (PSH+ACK) between the bot and the CnC server. Here, PSH refers to a push message and ACK refers to acknowledgement. Since the keep-alive messages are sent at regular intervals, one can observe periodic spikes in the bot-CnC traffic rate. The transmission of bot scanning packets is illustrated in Fig. 7. As can be observed, the scanning packets are sometimes transmitted within short intervals and at other times they are transmitted far apart, resembling a Poisson process.

In the next experiment, we commanded few infected bots to attack the victim server with UDP flood traffic which reaches a rate of 48K pps (packets per second). The attack does not wait for ICMP (Internet Control Message Protocol) reply packets (such as destination unreachable) to be sent back by the victim server. One of the non-IoT nodes in the testbed was configured as a UDP client. Once the victim server was overwhelmed, it started dropping legitimate UDP requests from the client. This can be noted from Fig. 8 which depicts the client UDP connection packet capture after the attack.

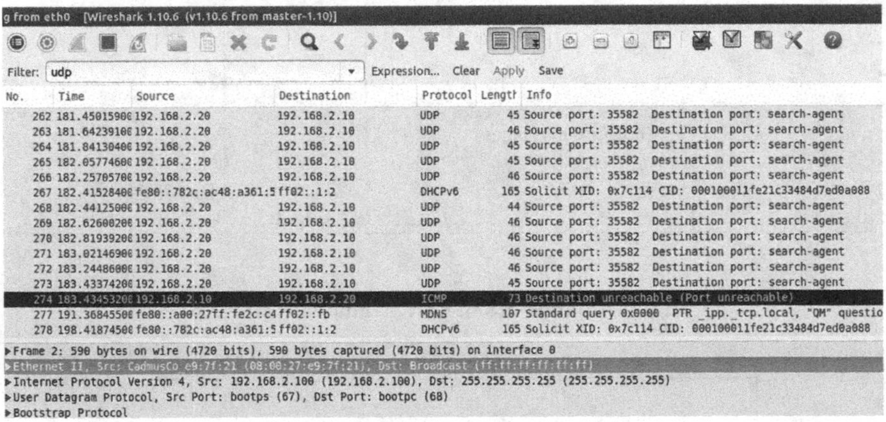

Fig. 8. Client UDP connection packet capture after UDP flood attack

We also conducted a TCP SYN flooding attack in which $\approx$46K pps were transmitted by the bots without listening for SYN-ACK packets sent back by the victim server. During the attack, the victim server encountered congestion as can be inferred from Fig. 9. It started sending out duplicate ACKs and retransmits packets multiple times which stop once the attack is over. This resulted in a denial of service to the benign TCP traffic from the client.

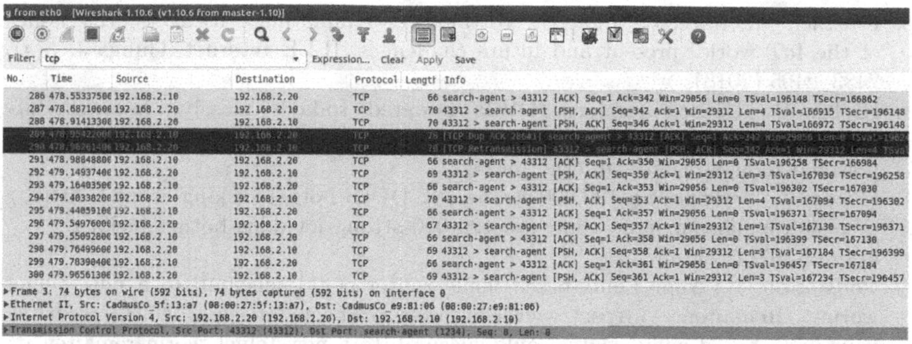

Fig. 9. Client TCP connection packet capture after SYN flood attack

5   Conclusion

In this paper, we presented a DETERlab-based IoT botnet testbed built within a secure contained environment with ancillary services such as DHCP, DNS and botnet infrastructure comprising of CnC and scanListen/loading servers. We described the setup process for various components of the testbed and associated challenges. The main features of the testbed were also listed. Finally, we ran some basic experiments and discussed the results showing bot-CnC communication, scanning traffic and few DDoS attacks which demonstrated the capabilities of our testbed.

Acknowledgment. The authors would like to appreciate the National Cybersecurity R&D Lab, Singapore for allowing us to use their testbed to collect important data which has been used in our work. This research is supported by the National Research Foundation, Prime Minister's Office, Singapore under its Corporate Laboratory@University Scheme, National University of Singapore, and Singapore Telecommunications Ltd.

References

1. Al-Fuqaha, A., Guizani, M., Mohammadi, M., Aledhari, M., Ayyash, M.: Internet of Things: a survey on enabling technologies, protocols, and applications. IEEE Commun. Surv. Tutor. **17**(4), 2347–2376 (2015)
2. Nordrum, A.: Popular Internet of Things forecast of 50 billion devices by 2020 is outdated. https://spectrum.ieee.org/tech-talk/telecom/internet/popular-internet-of-things-forecast-of-50-billion-devices-by-2020-is-outdated
3. Yang, Y., Wu, L., Yin, G., Li, L., Zhao, H.: A survey on security and privacy issues in Internet-of-Things. IEEE Internet Things J. **4**(5), 1250–1258 (2017)
4. Lin, J., Yu, W., Zhang, N., Yang, X., Zhang, H., Zhao, W.: A survey on Internet of Things: architecture, enabling technologies, security and privacy, and applications. IEEE Internet Things J. **4**(5), 1125–1142 (2017)

5. Frustaci, M., Pace, P., Aloi, G., Fortino, G.: Evaluating critical security issues of the IoT world: present and future challenges. IEEE Internet Things J. **5**(4), 2483–2495 (2018)
6. Krebs, B.: Hacked cameras, DVRs powered today's massive internet outage, October 2016. https://krebsonsecurity.com/2016/10/hacked-cameras-dvrs-powered-todays-massive-internet-outage/
7. Cimpanu, C.: There's a 120,000-strong IoT DDoS botnet lurking around. http://news.softpedia.com/news/there-s-a-120-000-strong-iot-ddos-botnet-lurking-around-507773.shtml
8. Constantin, L.: Your Linux-based home router could succumb to a new Telnet worm, Remaiten. https://www.computerworld.com/article/3049982/security/your-linux-based-home-router-could-succumb-to-a-new-telnet-worm-remaiten.html
9. Grange, W.: Hajime worm battles Mirai for control of the Internet of Things. https://www.symantec.com/connect/blogs/hajime-worm-battles-mirai-control-internet-things
10. Arghire, I.: IoT botnet used in website hacking attacks. https://www.securityweek.com/iot-botnet-used-website-hacking-attacks
11. Beek, C.: Mirai botnet creates army of IoT Orcs. https://securingtomorrow.mcafee.com/mcafee-labs/mirai-botnet-creates-army-iot-orcs/
12. Ilascu, I.: Mirai code still runs on many IoT devices. https://www.bitdefender.com/box/blog/iot-news/mirai-code-still-runs-many-iot-devices/
13. Calvet, J., et al.: The case for in-the-lab botnet experimentation: creating and taking down a 3000-node botnet. In: Proceedings of the 26th Annual Computer Security Applications Conference, ACSAC 2010, New York, pp. 141–150 (2010)
14. NCL: National Cybersecurity R&D Lab. https://ncl.sg/
15. DeterLab: Cyber-defense technology experimental research laboratory. https://www.isi.deterlab.net/index.php3
16. Barford, P., Blodgett, M.: Toward botnet Mesocosms. In: Proceedings of the First Conference on First Workshop on Hot Topics in Understanding Botnets, HotBots 2007, Berkeley, p. 6. USENIX Association (2007)
17. Jackson, A.W., Lapsley, D., Jones, C., Zatko, M., Golubitsky, C., Strayer, W.T.: SLINGbot: a system for live investigation of next generation botnets. In: Cybersecurity Applications Technology Conference for Homeland Security, pp. 313–318, March 2009
18. Vanderveen, K.B., et al.: Large-scale botnet analysis on a budget (2011)
19. Kreibich, C., Weaver, N., Kanich, C., Cui, W., Paxson, V.: GQ: practical containment for measuring modern malware systems. In: Proceedings of the 2011 ACM SIGCOMM Conference on Internet Measurement Conference, IMC 2011, New York, pp. 397–412. ACM (2011)
20. ElSheikh, M.H., Gadelrab, M.S., Ghoneim, M.A., Rashwan, M.: Botgen: a new approach for in-lab generation of botnet datasets. In: 9th International Conference on Malicious and Unwanted Software: The Americas (MALWARE), pp. 76–84, October 2014
21. Alomari, E., Manickam, S., Gupta, B.B., Singh, P., Anbar, M.: Design, deployment and use of HTTP-based botnet (HBB) testbed. In: 16th International Conference on Advanced Communication Technology, pp. 1265–1269, February 2014
22. Ahmad, M.A., Woodhead, S., Gan, D.: The V-network testbed for malware analysis. In: International Conference on Advanced Communication Control and Computing Technologies (ICACCCT), pp. 629–635, May 2016

23. Kolias, C., Kambourakis, G., Stavrou, A., Voas, J.: DDoS in the IoT: Mirai and other botnets. Computer **50**(7), 80–84 (2017)
24. MySQL: The world's most popular open source database. https://www.mysql.com/
25. Winward, R.: Mirai: inside of an IoT Botnet, February 2017. https://www.nanog.org/sites/default/files/1_Winward_Mirai_The_Rise.pdf
26. Bellard, F.: QEMU, a fast and portable dynamic translator. In: Proceedings of the Annual Conference on USENIX Annual Technical Conference, ATEC 2005, Berkeley, p. 41. USENIX Association (2005). https://www.qemu.org/

Knowledge Graph

Capturing Domain Knowledge Through Extensible Components

Erik Kline, Genevieve Bartlett[✉], Geoff Lawler, Robert Story, and Michael Elkins

Information Sciences Institute, University of Southern California, Los Angeles, USA
{ekline,bartlett,glawler,rstory,elkins}@isi.edu
http://www.isi.edu

Abstract. Recreating real-world network scenarios on testbeds is common in validating security solutions, but modeling networks correctly requires a good deal of expertise in multiple domains. A testbed user must understand the solution being validated, the real-world deployment environments, in addition to understanding what features in these environments matter and how to model these features correctly in a testbed. As real-world scenarios and the security solutions we design become more diverse and complex, it becomes less likely that the testbed user is able to be a domain expert in their technology, a field expert in the deploy environments for their technology, and an expert in how to model these environments on the testbed. Without the proper expertise from multiple domains, testbed users produce overly simplified and inappropriate test environments, which do not provide adequate validation. To address this pressing need to share domain knowledge in the testbed community, we introduce our Extensible Components Framework for testbed network modeling. Our framework enables multiple experts to contribute to a complex network model without needing to explicitly collaborate or translate between domains. The fundamental goal of our Extensible Components is to capture the knowledge of domain experts and turn this knowledge into off-the-shelf models that end-users can easily utilize as first-class testbed objects. We demonstrate the design and use of our Extensible Components Framework through implementing Click Modular Router [10] based Extensible Components on the DETER testbed, and advocate that our framework can be applied to other environments. We focus on *wired* network models, but outline how Extensible Components can be used to model other types of networks such as wireless. (This material is based on research sponsored by DARPA under agreement number HR0011-15-C-0096. The U.S. Government is authorized to reproduce and distribute reprints for Governmental purposes notwithstanding any copyright notation thereon. The views and conclusions contained herein are those of the authors and should not be interpreted as necessarily representing the official policies or endorsements, either expressed or implied, of DARPA or the U.S. Government.)

© ICST Institute for Computer Sciences, Social Informatics and Telecommunications Engineering 2019
Published by Springer Nature Switzerland AG 2019. All Rights Reserved
H. Gao et al. (Eds.): TridentCom 2018, LNICST 270, pp. 141–156, 2019.
https://doi.org/10.1007/978-3-030-12971-2_9

Keywords: Testbed validation · Network models ·
Knowledge capture · Network testbed · Testbed experimentation

1   Introduction

Validation of security and networking solutions requires creating and harnessing complex scenarios and realizing those scenarios on a testbed infrastructure. A testbed user must decide what aspects of a real-world environment play a role in validation and determine how to map these real environment features into the testbed environment correctly. Proper validation requires a deep understanding and meaningful expertise across multiple domains [7]. Specifically, to perform proper validation with today's technology, a testbed user must maintain expertise across three distinct domains: First, a testbed user must understand the solution being validated. Second, she must understand the real-world environments where the solution will be deployed. Last, the user must understand what features are relevant in these environments and how to model these features correctly in a testbed. As the real-world has grown increasingly more diverse and complex, the burden on the testbed user has grown immensely. It has become less and less likely that a testbed user can maintain being a domain expert in her technology, a field expert in the deploy environments for her technology, and an expert in how to model these environments on the testbed. In lieu of working with field and modeling experts, testbed users often produce overly simplified test environments, or use canned modeling approaches unsuitable for their experiment which do not provide adequate realism for testing and validation.

Collaborating with field and modeling experts reduces the burden on the testbed user while working towards more realistic testing scenarios, but such a collaboration requires a good deal of effort to translate expertise between domains. Ad-hoc translation between domains can be tedious and without structured *knowledge capture*, the time spent sharing expertise to build testbed models has little pay-off beyond the initial effort. Low-effort knowledge capture to facilitate reuse, sharing and repeatability is thus a common goal in testbed validation.

In this paper, we describe our work to perform knowledge capture and domain expertise translation in testbed network modeling for experimental validation. We achieve this knowledge capture through a framework we call the *Extensible Components Framework*. A key feature of our Extensible Components is the capture and dissemination of knowledge at three distinct levels—the model approach, the model specification and how to composed this model into a larger network model. Further, we treat Extensible Components as first-class testbed objects. That is, the testbed understands what an Extensible Component is and how to allocate and instantiate one given an experiment configuration. First-class status for Extensible Component allows experimenters to easily deploy and use complex models and scenarios without having to gain significant knowledge on the components implementation, modeling approach or configuration.

We describe the three expert domains our Extensible Components Framework brings together through knowledge capture (Sect. 2). We then discuss how to: create an Extensible Component (Sect. 3.1), extend the component by specifying resident models (Sect. 3.2), and how end-users easily use, combine and share these models (Sect. 3.3). We follow with example components of a wired network (Sect. 4.1) and wireless network (Sect. 4.2) and include a brief discussion on our experiences with users and experts using our Extensible Components. We close by discussing related work and how our Extensible Components Framework can incorporate many existing tools. Our initial implementation and use of our framework is freely available and currently implemented on the DETER testbed [11]. We discuss the straightforward process of porting to other testbed platforms in Sect. 3.4.

2   Extensible Components

The fundamental goal of our Extensible Components Framework is to be able to capture the knowledge of domain experts and turn this knowledge into off-the-shelf models that end-users can easily utilize.

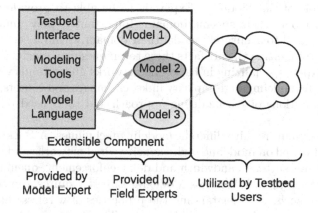

Fig. 1. Extensible component overview

We capture and disseminate domain expertise from three distinct experts—Modeling Experts, Field Experts and Users. A Modeling Expert builds tools that accurately model a specific domain, providing the *ability to model* their domain on a testbed to others. This ability to model is the core of an Extensible Component. Field Experts then extend an Extensible Component by building multiple specific models of their domain. Finally, users compose these specific models to build aggregate networking models which they can experiment upon, reuse and share with others. An overview of how this information is captured, provided and shared is illustrated in Fig. 1 while the propagation of information is shown in Fig. 2.

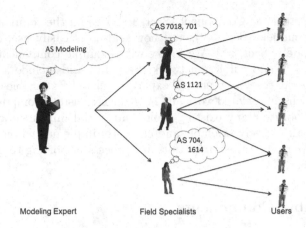

Fig. 2. The three levels of knowledge capture and how knowledge propagates

2.1 Modeling Experts and Languages

The critical role of the Modeling Expert is to be able to provide others with the ability to model their specific domain. Importantly, they understand the techniques required to accurately model their domain within a set of given constraints while recognizing the artifacts these techniques may create. For example, a Modeling Expert specializing in backbone networks understands what features are important in modeling high capacity links, exchanges and routers, and understands the limitations of his modeling approach and tools used to realize this approach.

Different domains require different modeling techniques. A Backbone Modeling Expert is focused on modeling high-capacity wired networks and understands modeling features such as bandwidth and delay enforcement, queuing strategies and routing techniques. A Wireless Modeling Expert requires knowledge of different features, such as understanding the properties of wireless channel access strategies, wireless collisions, and hidden nodes. The Backbone Modeling Expert does not care about nor know how to model the concerns of the Wireless Expert and vice versa.

Importantly, multiple Modeling Experts and modeling approaches can exist for the same domain. Different model approaches make different trade-offs between resources and fidelity, modeling certain features with high-fidelity and reducing fidelity in other aspects. For example, one could model Autonomous System (AS) networks using a link-centric approach or a router-centric approach. A link-centric approach provides high fidelity modeling of link properties and congestion while providing relaxed fidelity for modeling of routers and routing protocols. Conversely, a router-centric approach offers a high fidelity model of routers and routing protocols while abstracting many of the link properties, which may be more appropriate than a link-centric approach for testing new routing protocols. Both of these experts are modeling ASes but their approaches provide different trade-offs for experimenters. Supporting diversity in modeling approaches enables broader applicability, as not all experiments require the same level of fidelity in all features.

The Modeling Expert can also provide controls on the amount of information that may be visible through her modeling tools. An example of this would be a model of an AS which does not leak any topological information to the edge users, similar to the current Internet. This ability to provide privacy is important for Field Experts who want to create models for others to test against, but do not want to expose any proprietary information about their structure. Conversely, a Modeling Expert may not provide these guarantees where they cannot be enforced or do not make sense to enforce. For example, a model approach for an AS may have to expose topological information when testing new routing protocols in order make validation guarantees. In both cases, the Modeling Expert can pass down this knowledge of constraints to Field Experts to ensure Field Experts and Users understand the privacy and fidelity guarantees.

Beyond providing tools and an approach to properly model a domain, Modeling Experts must also provide an easy way for others to customize and create specific models using their tools and modeling approach. For this, we advocate adoption of small languages that can easily and accurately describe and set the features of a model. Using a language to describe a model, rather than parameterizing a blob of code, provides flexibility and scaling, such as using loops to create and set multiple parts of a model. For example, an AS model may be described with a simple edge-list link language that provides an easy description of a network and its link properties. Similarly, a wireless model may utilize a node-list approach that describes the position of speakers, their mobility and their transmission capabilities. Whatever language is chosen, the goal is for the language to easily describe a model, without requiring the person describing the specific model to understand the underlying model implementation or even the modeling approach—beyond just a broad understanding its goals and limitations.

Finally, to provide others with a general idea of a component's applicability, Modeling Experts need to provide some documentation. This documentation should give a brief and high-level description of the overall modeling approach, and the capabilities and constraints of the model, allowing Field Experts and Users to make informed decisions when choosing a component.

2.2   Models and Field Experts

After a Modeling Expert provides the ability to create and exercise a model, it falls upon Field Experts to extend components by generating models. Field Experts have significant knowledge in their relevant field but may not have knowledge of *how* to model their domain. For example, an operator of an AS knows the properties of their links and structure of their topology but may not know how to accurately represent that on a testbed. Instead of learning how to model, the Field Experts simply utilize the languages provided by a Modeling Expert to describe their system and generate a model of it on the testbed.

Of course, Modeling Experts and Field Experts are not mutually exclusive. Often a Modeling Expert will have significant knowledge about one or more fields, and a Field Expert may know how to approach testbed modeling. However, we expect that there are significantly more Field Experts than Modeling Experts, as accurately modeling systems is a difficult challenge and a niche area of expertise. Thus, it makes sense to capture and amplify a Modeling Expert's knowledge.

Just as Users can compose models into a larger network model, Field Experts can also draw on multiple Extensible Components and are not required to use only one Modeling Expert's approach. For example, an AS Field Expert may want to represent her system using multiple models—a link-centric model, a router-centric model and a hybrid model. As long as the Field Expert can understand the trade-offs, as accurately described by the Modeling Expert, she can make rational and intelligent decisions about which Extensible Components to use.

Ultimately, the goal of the Field Expert is to generate models through the Modeling Experts tools, and provide those models to users who can run experiments using these models. It is incumbent on the Field Experts to select the Extensible Components they feel adequately describe their domains while also meeting their privacy concerns as described in Sect. 2.1. Further access controls for these models can be provided and enforced by the testbed.

2.3   Users

Users are the final level of our three-level approach, and are the ultimate recipient of the captured knowledge in our Extensible Components Framework. The fundamental goal of extensible components is to allow experimenters to utilize complex network systems within their experiments without having to obtain domain knowledge of a specific field or modeling approach. Building on knowledge from Modeling and Field Experts, the User can now simply grab one or more of the provided models and begin to experiment against them. The User does not need to understand how the model is implemented, or the structure of the model itself, in order to conduct an experiment. All the User needs to know is the goal of a model and what constraints and artifacts may occur by utilizing this model. With this information, the User can conduct complex and scientifically valid experiments without spending the tedious time becoming a domain expert in modeling or deployment environments.

3   Component Lifecycle

In the previous section we described how an Extensible Component brings together expertise from Modeling and Field Experts to unburden the testbed user and promote reuse. Next we describe the details of how a component is created and used. We have developed and used our Extensible Component prototypes on the DETER testbed [11], but believe porting our components to other testbeds would be a straightforward process.

3.1   Creating a Component

In order to create a new component, the Modeling Expert is required to provide three building blocks—a small language, a tool or set of tools to realize the component, and an interface to generate and exercise the component. As discussed in Sect. 2.1, the language is utilized by Field Experts to describe a model. We provide no restrictions on the choice of language, providing flexibility to the Modeling Expert to choose whatever best suits their tools. The expert is free to utilize languages that already exist if that is the best option.

The tool created by the Modeling Expert receives models specified in the component's language, and instantiates a functional component representing that model as output. The choice of tool is once again up to the Modeling Expert. Testbeds, such as DETER, can provide canned capabilities, such that the expert may only need to translate their language into one that a canned capability already understands. For example, one of the components we've created for DETER uses the Click Modular Router [10] as it's underlying implementation. Thus, our component tool translates our modeling language into a configuration file that Click understands.

The final building block needed to be able to create and utilize a new component is an interface to the testbed that allows the component to be allocated and instantiated as a first-class object. For DETER, this is a TCL (NS) interface. We provide Modeling Experts with a TCL library that they can import and build off of to provide their interface. These experts simply need to sub-class the component class and then implement the abstracted functions. These functions are 'create' and 'add-link' which indicate to the testbed how many nodes to allocate to the component and how to connect other testbed objects to this component. Further, the component class accepts an arbitrary number of arguments to be passed to the sub-class, allowing Modeling Experts to accept variability during the component construction.

```
set myc [$ns component ASWAN AS701]
```

Fig. 3. Example component instantiation

Figure 3 shows the basic Extensible Component API as supplied by the component library. This example tells DETER to allocate a new component which is of type ASWAN (a component for modeling an Autonomous System Wide Area Networks). Everything else will be passed to the component creation method to be handled by the specific component sub-class. Thus, in this example, our Modeling Expert created a component called ASWAN, which expects a single argument, the specific model to instantiate. The specific model, AS701, is created and named by the Field Expert (and models a specific Autonomous System's network environment).

3.2   Creating a Model

The complexity of creating a new component allows for the rest of the framework to be significantly simpler. To create a model, the Field Expert simply needs to pick a component and utilize the given language to express the model. The challenge for the Field Expert is picking a component that can adequately express their model while also understanding the components capabilities, constraints and potential artifacts. For example, a component that models ASes in a link-centric fashion may have a maximum number of links per CPU it can model before some artifacting occurs. The Modeling Expert documents what these constraints and limits, and the Field Expert must heed the documentation to create useful and accurate models.

```
11 12 {"bw": "400Mbps",
       "delay": "10ms",
       "loss": "0.0001"}
11 13 {"bw": "200Mbps",
       "delay": "15ms",
       "loss": "0.0001"}
```

Fig. 4. Small example of a modeling language

Once the component has been chosen, the expert creates their model within the Extensible Component's language. The code segment in Fig. 4 is an example of a link-centric modeling language using an edge list format. The Field Expert has used this language to describe a modeled network with three routers and two edges (links "11"–"12" and "11"–"13"), with several link constraints specified for each edge. Once the model has been specified, it is imported into an archive or library. On DETER, the models are given a name and stored in a model repository for later use.

3.3   Using a Component

Utilizing an Extensible Component within an experiment is where everything comes together. First, the interface created by the Modeling Expert is exercised by the user to define, instantiate and deploy the component. On DETER, this involves importing the TCL library and defining the component within the topology as shown in Fig. 3. The user can pass any options to the component through this interface. Further, the user can connect the component to other experiment objects using the 'add-link' API, which exposes specific I/O portions of the component allowing the component to be physically linked to other experimental hardware. At this point, the user does not need to do anything additionally to have their component realized. When the experiment is instantiated, the component will be automatically configured, initialized and enabled.

3.4   Deploying Extensible Components on a Testbed

The majority of our discussion of Extensible Components has been based on
our deployment on the DETER testbed [11]. However, the overall framework
should be amenable to most testing infrastructures. To utilize our Extensible
Components Framework on any given testbed, three fundamental capabilities
are required. First, the infrastructure must be able to express a component
as a first-class object like any other object in that testbed. This means the
testbed back-end will deploy, connect and configure the relevant infrastructure to
instantiate the component. Second, a user must be able to express the component
within their experiment configuration. On DETER, this is accomplished via a
TCL (NS) library available to any user and other testbeds would require similar
modifications or extensions. Finally, a repository to store Extensible Components
and models generated by Modeling Experts and Field Experts, respectively, is
required so that the Extensible Components and models can be easily retrieved
and used by experimenters.

4   Experiences with Example Components

We have two example components in use that demonstrate the domain expertise
separation of our Extensible Components Framework and the capabilities of
Extensible Components. Both of these Extensible Components have been used to
make multiple models of real-world, toy example and corner-case testing models.

The first component, Wide area network (WAN) emulation, is freely available and has been used by multiple teams for testing and evaluation in a recent
DARPA program. The second component, wireless network emulation, is currently in development for a second DARPA program. Both of these components
currently use the same Click-based [10] back-end for realization. We are working
towards augmenting Click with additional tools to realize these components, as
other technologies are better suited to accurately model specific elements in each
domain. A key feature of our Extensible Components Framework is the separation of the component use from the model implementation. As we change the
underlying tools used to realize a model, the testbed user interface and configuration interface of the model can remain largely the same, reducing the burden
on testbed users and Field Experts.

4.1   Wide Area Network Emulation

Wide area network (WAN) emulation is a common need for testbed validation,
and typically requires accurate and realistic topologies. In over nearly a decade
of working with DETER, we observed that without easily accessible and usable
network emulation, experimenters utilize excessive testbed resources simulating
real-world topology. This network simulation approach is not an efficient use
of resources as each physical machine used for simulation typically acts as a
simple store and forward router, and provides nothing else to the experiment.

We needed a technology that would allow experimenters to utilize the domain knowledge of WAN operators without having to gain that knowledge themselves, while also being far more efficient in resource allocation.

To address this inefficient use of resources, we implemented a WAN Emulation Extensible Component. The WAN emulation component allows an experimenter to deploy an emulated WAN of multiple routers and links on a small number of physical resources (usually just one physical machine, but in complex topologies, this is expanded to more).

As researchers on modeling and testbeds, we were the Modeling Experts for the WAN Emulation Extensible Component. We created all three of the essential building blocks required in our Extensible Components Framework (as discussed in Sect. 3.1). Our component specifies an edge-list based modeling language, similar to that seen in Fig. 4, which allows Field Experts to describe routers and the links between them across multiple features. These include bandwidth, delay, multiple loss modeling approaches, multiple queuing strategies, AQM, packet reordering, random bit error as well as many others. The second building block is a tool that converts the model as described in the modeling language into a format that can be utilized by the testbed. To build this tool, we leveraged the existing Click [10] capabilities of DETER. Thus, our python-based tool simply translates our edge list into a Click configuration. This tool is exercised at experiment run-time, pulling the specified model from the model repository, translating it and instantiating Click.

Finally, we built additional TCL interfaces to allow users to exercise the component as a first-class testbed object. This interface is very simple, requiring the user to only specify the model they wish to instantiate. Further, the user is required to connect the models I/O interfaces to other network components. An example connection is shown in Fig. 6 which connects an experimental node called "mynode" to our component at an I/O location called "router1". This means that a physical link between mynode and our component will be constructed and the data from that link will enter the component's topology at router1.

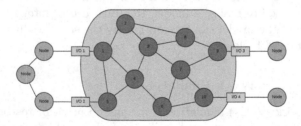

Fig. 5. Logical topology of our WAN with component in blue and other objects in orange. The square boxes represent I/O points where data enters and exits the component. (Color figure online)

An example testbed topology linking into a model from our WAN emulation component can be seen in Fig. 5. The highlighted blue area represents a WAN topology model. The four squares at the edge of this zone represent the I/O points where the testbed connects other objects to the component model. In this example, we connect four generic 'nodes' to the component model at the four given I/O locations. Data sent from these nodes to the component model traverse the given network, experiencing any network effects that are modeled, before exiting at another (or possibly the same) I/O point. Note that other testbed objects can exist that are not directly related to the component. We could connect other Extensible Components which encapsulate completely different modeling tools, or other physical nodes, or any other testbed object.

Since Extensible Components are first-class testbed objects, when the experiment is realized, the component is already correctly configured and operational, again reducing burden on the testbed user as there is no need to learn details of testbed operation in order to instantiate models. Importantly, a testbed user can specify an experiment with multiple models from one or more Extensible Components—all modeling different, and potentially complex, network systems which the testbed user can link together as needed.

Our WAN Extensible Component was used to generate multiple WAN models. To date, we have over 30 models associated with our Extensible Component, most of which were utilized in a recent DARPA program. The majority are models tailored to stress test and validate a particular system, or models designed to demo a feature of a system. A handful of these models capture Field Expert knowledge on military and commercial networks. We found capturing the knowledge of the operational Field Experts in the form of Extensible Component models greatly reduced the effort and time needed to get everyone within the DARPA program on the same page for testing, validation and demonstrations. The testbed users could focus on their systems and spent less time on understanding the details of the operational networks their systems would be deployed on and less time digging into the internals of the testbed.

While models are typically defined by the Field Experts, within the DARPA program we found it was also valuable to provide multiple dynamic controls directly to the testbed user. Our WAN Extensible Component allows users to tune very global and very specific link-level properties during an experiment, enabling testbed users to customize testing for stress testing and corner-case testing.

```
set link1 [$ns duplex-link
           $mynode [$myc entry router1]
           1000Mb 0.0ms DropTail]
```

Fig. 6. Connecting a component

Current Implementation Performance. As the Modeling Experts for wide area networks, it is our responsibility to describe the capabilities and limitations of our Extensible Component. As a link-based model of a WAN, the capabilities are well understood—the component enables modeling link properties with high-fidelity. The artifacts of these capabilities are also well understood, though are complex to express. For example, how bandwidth shaping is conducted on a link can greatly vary the effects on a flow. Token bucket approaches can cause unexpected burstiness where as dynamic queues based on bandwidth and delay result in less burstiness but can be more resource intensive (reducing the overall throughput available). We have quantified many of these capabilities and limitations for a multitude of our link properties.

Understanding the fundamental limitations of the underlying back-end is also critical. To this end, we measured the packet per second (PPS) performance of our Click-based [10] back-end under a variety of scenarios using 72 byte packets. All our experiments were conducted on a dual CPU, 12 Core Intel Xeon CPU E5-2650 v4 at 2.20 GHz with 64 GBs of RAM and two 40 Gigabit Intel XL710 interface cards. To achieve best performance, we deployed our system using DPDK [13] and FastClick [3].

First, we obtained an upper bound on performance—the maximum PPS Click could process. Utilizing a queueless Click configuration, we paired each interface and achieved 36 million PPS per NUMA node on our hardware (a total of 72 million PPS). This may not be a true upper bound, as our traffic generation nodes cannot generate additional traffic. This still represents a useful practical upper bound, as our link-based modeling approach requires queues to accurately emulate multiple link properties. Queues represent a significant performance penalty, as they act as a point where threads context switch and move to process each packet. Simply enabling basic queuing reduced our performance by 90% to 4 million PPS per NUMA node. Fortunately, adding all of our other link emulation options had a negligible effect on performance.

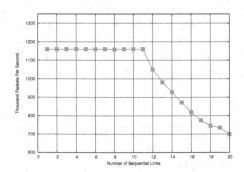

Fig. 7. Packets per second (PPS) throughput performance as we add additional sequential links in our WAN model.

It is also necessary to understand the performance of each emulated link. As each link can only be serviced by one thread at a time[1], there is a fundamental limit to how many packets a single link can process. Our experiments determined that an individual link can handle 1.2 million PPS. Further, placing multiple links in sequence has no effect on performance until twelve sequential links, after-which there is a steady decrease in performance. Figure 7 depicts this eventual decline in PPS as we add additional sequential links. This reduction in performance is most likely caused by thread contention and unexpected queuing delay throughout the sequential pipeline. As Modeling Experts, we must make it clear to any Field Experts that sequential links that do not have any branching points are best modeled as one single link.

The final performance question to ask is how many parallel links can be modeled before we experience artifacting. On our test setup, we have currently modeled up to 150 parallel links without experiencing loss of performance and are continuing to push this number until we begin to reach our limitations. It is also important to realize that placing bandwidth limitations on a link may reduce the effect of performance reductions. As a caveat, our results are directly related to the hardware tested on, and better hardware will have better performance.

4.2   Wireless Networks

Modeling wireless networks is vastly different than modeling wired networks. As part of a current DARPA program, we are in the process of developing a wireless emulation capability using Extensible Components. As modeling experts, we need to provide a modeling language for this component. The language is different than that of our WAN component as the notion of links does transfer to a broadcast medium. We are exploring a node-based, rather than edge-based, format that specifies the position, mobility, and transmission strength of our wireless speakers, amongst other properties.

As described previously, a tool is required to translate from our modeling language to a realization on the testbed. Further, a new back-end engine will be required to be able to conduct this realization. We are currently in construction of this back-end which focuses heavily on the network layer aspects of wireless, although many of the physical layer considerations are also being added in. Several critical constraints, such as bandwidth, delay and loss, are of course being developed. Additional capabilities are also being added including wireless collisions, channel access strategies and hidden terminals.

For modeling approaches of our Extensible Component, we are exploring a wide range of existing implementations that could be leveraged, including modifying Click [10], CORE [1], EMANE [14] or a combined integration (e.g. [2]). Until the back-end is fully realized, we will not be ready to develop our translation tool. However, understanding what can be modeled based on our language and our back-end heavily informs the capabilities of the overall system.

---

[1] This limit is important to prevent unexpected packet reordering or costly resequencing.

The final necessary building block for this new Extensible Component is the testbed interface. This portion is perhaps the simplest, as many of the relevant capabilities already exist in our library on DETER and our other existing components. To realize this new component, we need to make sure our new interface can accurately instantiate and realize the component on the testbed when the experiment becomes available. As stated previously, this is critical to ensure components remain first-class objects and are, therefore, easily usable for experimenters.

5   Related Work

Our work is related and motivated by a large body of research in network simulation and emulation. Many of these works offer tools which can be used in our Extensible Component Framework, and we expect to expand our model definitions beyond Click [10].

Network simulators, such as NS2/3 and OPNET [5] are widely used today. While tools like OPNET, share our goals in providing composable models to users, the extensibility of such tools is limited as these tools are largely focused on simulating an entire network, including using simulated traffic on a single piece of hardware, severely limiting how models built on these tools can interconnect. The ability to define a model across simulated *and* emulated components in these frameworks is limited. Likewise, network emulation tools such as Netem [8] and Dummynet [4] are focused on emulation, and lack the ability to define a model across both emulation and simulation. Later generations of NS and OPNET added "system-in-the-loop" capabilities, allowing traffic generated on external and real systems to be piped through the simulation. Despite system-in-the-loop capabilities, and a huge library of expert defined models, the ability to link OPNET models into a network of other models outside of the OPNET ecosystem is limited. Tools like NS3 and Dummynet offer enough flexibility to define composable components which can link into a range of other simulated or emulated components, but these tools still require a framework to capture complex models and incorporate field expertise.

Tools such as Emulab's NS Emulation (NSE) based on NS [6] and the U.S. Naval Research Laboratory's Common Open Research Emulator (CORE) [1] provide the ability to define a mix of simulation and emulation network components across a set of testbed resources. NSE's base-components are primitive and require additional framework to capture a complex model. NSE is no longer supported, but is an example of a toolkit which can easily benefit from our Extensible Components Framework. CORE [1] provides a 'network lab in a box' with a strong and usable API and an informative GUI. CORE still requires the user to have a good deal of domain knowledge on the networks being modeled as well as significant knowledge on the operation of CORE. CORE would be highly useful as a Extensible Component itself, which could be deployed through our framework to transfer domain knowledge from CORE experts to average experimenters.

Lastly, the Network Modeling and Simulation Environment (NEMSE) [9] works to provide unified access to a large number of emulation and simulation tools on the Emulab testbed platform [12], including CORE [1], OPNET [5] and Click [3,10]. While unified tool access is an important step towards sharing models, NEMSE lacks a framework to define complex and composable models and does not address treating models as first-class objects on its chosen testbed platform.

6 Conclusion

Complex and realistic scenarios are required to accurately evaluate and validate security and networking solutions. The knowledge required to generate faithful models continues to expand as the complexity of these systems and their environments grows. It is unrealistic to expect an experimenter will have or be able to obtain the necessary cross-domain expertise to generate these models and conduct scientifically valid experiments. Therefore, we must reduce the burden on these experimenters by capturing the knowledge of domain experts and disseminating this knowledge through first-class experimental objects to end-users.

In this paper, we described our Extensible Components Framework to perform knowledge capture and domain expertise transfer. A key realization incorporated into our framework is that knowledge should be captured and disseminated at three distinct levels—the modeling approach, the model creation and the model utilization. This separation allows knowledge to be captured by those who know how to describe their domain without necessarily knowing how to implement a model for their domain (Field Experts), as well as those who know how to accurately model a domain, but do not know the specifics of real-world networks and layouts (Modeling Experts). Further, all of this captured knowledge can be made available and usable to an experimenter without needing to obtain that domain knowledge. By treating Extensible Components as first-class testbed objects, experimenters can easily deploy and use complex models and scenarios without having to gain additional knowledge on the components implementation or configuration. It is our belief that this framework will promote rigorous experimentation and validation of security and networking systems by promoting the creation and sharing of accurate models.

References

1. Ahrenholz, J.: Comparison of CORE network emulation platforms. In: Military Communications Conference, 2010 - MILCOM 2010, pp. 166–171, October 2010. https://doi.org/10.1109/MILCOM.2010.5680218
2. Ahrenholz, J., Goff, T., Adamson, B.: Integration of the core and emane network emulators. In: 2011 - MILCOM 2011 Military Communications Conference, pp. 1870–1875, November 2011. https://doi.org/10.1109/MILCOM.2011.6127585
3. Barbette, T., Soldani, C., Mathy, L.: Fast userspace packet processing. In: Proceedings of the Eleventh ACM/IEEE Symposium on Architectures for Networking and Communications Systems, ANCS 2015, pp. 5–16. IEEE Computer Society, Washington (2015). http://dl.acm.org/citation.cfm?id=2772722.2772727

4. Carbone, M., Rizzo, L.: Dummynet revisited. ACM SIGCOMM Comput. Commun. Rev. **40**(2), 12–20 (2010). https://doi.org/10.1145/1764873.1764876
5. Chang, X.: Network simulations with OPNET. In: Proceedings of the 31st Conference on Winter Simulation: Simulation–A Bridge to the Future, WSC 1999, vol. 1, pp. 307–314. ACM, New York (1999). https://doi.org/10.1145/324138.324232
6. Fall, K.: Network emulation in the Vint/NS simulator. In: Proceedings of the fourth IEEE Symposium on Computers and Communications, pp. 244–250 (1999)
7. Floyd, S., Kohler, E.: Internet research needs better models. ACM SIGCOMM Comput. Commun. Rev. **33**(1), 29–34 (2003). https://doi.org/10.1145/774763.774767
8. Hemminger, S.: Network Emulation with NetEm. In: Linux Conf AU (2005). http://www.linux.org.au/conf/2005/abstract2e37.html?id=163
9. Hench, D.L.: Complex network modeling with an Emulab HPC. In: Proceedings of the 16th Annual IEEE High Performance Extreme Computing Conference (HPEC 2012), September 2012
10. Kohler, E., Morris, R., Chen, B., Jannotti, J., Kaashoek, M.F.: The click modular router. ACM Trans. Comput. Syst. **18**(3), 263–297 (2000). https://doi.org/10.1145/354871.354874
11. Mirkovic, J., Benzel, T.V., Faber, T., Braden, R., Wroclawski, J.T., Schwab, S.: The DETER project: advancing the science of cyber security experimentation and test. In: 2010 IEEE International Conference on Technologies for Homeland Security (HST), pp. 1–7, November 2010. https://doi.org/10.1109/THS.2010.5655108
12. White, B., et al.: An integrated experimental environment for distributed systems and networks. In: Proceedings of the Operating System Design and Implementation, pp. 255–270 (2002)
13. DPDK: Data Plane Development Kit. https://dpdk.org/
14. Extendable Mobile Ad-hoc Network Emulator (EMANE). https://www.nrl.navy.mil/itd/ncs/products/emane

Formalizing DIKW Architecture for Modeling Security and Privacy as Typed Resources

Yucong Duan[1], Lougao Zhan[1], Xinyue Zhang[1],
and Yuanyuan Zhang[2(✉)]

[1] College of Information Science and Technology,
Hainan University, Haikou, China
duanyucong@hotmail.com, 2286345869@qq.com,
yuexinaai@163.com
[2] College of Information Technology,
Zhejiang Chinese Medical University, Hangzhou, China
zyy@zjtcm.net

Abstract. Currently the content of security protection has been expanded multiple sources. The security protection especially of the implicit content from multiple sources poses new challenges to the collection, identification, customization of protection strategies, modeling, etc. We are enlightened by the potential of DIKW (Data, Information, Knowledge, Wisdom) architecture to express semantic of natural language content and human intention. But currently there lacks formalized semantics for the DIKW architecture by itself which poses a challenge for building conceptual models on top of this architecture. We proposed a formalization of the elements of DIKW. The formalization centers the ideology of modeling Data as multiple dimensional hierarchical Types related to observable existence of the Sameness, Information as identification of Data with explicit Difference, Knowledge as applying Completeness of the Type, and Wisdom as variability prediction. Based on this formalization, we propose a solution framework for security concerns centering Type transitions in Graph, Information Graph and Knowledge Graph.

Keywords: Typed resources · Data, Information, Knowledge, Wisdom

1 Introduction

From the view of the forming process of a software requirement, individuals express their security and privacy concerns [15] in natural language specifications as a start. Currently the content of security protection has been expanded to multiple sources. The security protection especially of the implicit content from multiple sources poses new challenges to the collection, identification, customization of protection strategies, modeling, etc. We are enlightened by the potential of DIKW (Data, Information, Knowledge, Wisdom) architecture to express semantic of natural language content and human intention. Towards tackling the challenge of the complexity originating in the interleaving and association of crosscutting compositions in specification and models, we propose to categorize content objects and relationships uniformly as typed DIKW

H. Gao et al. (Eds.): TridentCom 2018, LNICST 270, pp. 157–168, 2019.
https://doi.org/10.1007/978-3-030-12971-2_10

content. But currently there lacks formalized semantics for the DIKW architecture by itself which poses a challenge for building conceptual models on top of this architecture.

We proposed a formalization of the elements of DIKW. The formalization centers the ideology of modeling Data as multiple dimensional hierarchical Types related to observable existence of the Sameness, Information as identification of Data with explicit Difference, Knowledge as applying Completeness of the Type, and Wisdom as variability prediction. Based on this formalization, we propose a solution framework for security concerns centering Type transitions in Graph, Information Graph and Knowledge Graph [13, 14]. We further categorize target resources of data and information according to their presence in searching space as explicit and implicit [2]. Corresponding security protection schemes are constructed according to the conversion and search cost differences corresponding to different types of resource expressions. These schemes support the design and provision of Value Driven [9] security solutions based on the differences of the conversion cost of different types of resources and the search cost after conversion.

Zins [4] illustrated the concepts of defining data, information and knowledge. Duan et al. [13] clarified the architecture of Knowledge Graph in terms of data, information, knowledge and wisdom. Chen et al. proposed visualization of data information and knowledge [3]. Work [1, 6] proposed to recover implicit information through abductive inference. Hundepool et al. propose to make useful inferences from groups while preserving the privacy of individuals [7]. Soria-Comas et al. [12] present ideas that privacy degree is in proportion to the amount of linkability. McSherry et al. [10] focus on sequential composition and parallel composition in composability properties.

2 Definitions in Typed DIKW Architecture

2.1 Existing Concepts of Content

To layout an uniform conceptual target of discussion, we define all content in a system description as resources regardless of whether it expresses static semantics or dynamic semantics.

Target of discussion:
Resources::=<content$_{static}$, content$_{dynamic}$>

Static content represents individual elements or facts, or expresses structural relationships among elements or structures. By structural relationship, we mean relationships (REL) of which the represented semantic meaning by them doesn't represent a meaningful temporal or asymmetric logical order. We denote structural relationships as reversible relationship, and denote temporal or asymmetric logical relationships as irreversible relationships.

REL::=<REL$_{reversible}$, REL$_{irreversible}$>
content$_{static}$::=<{REL$_{reversible}$}*, {element}*>
Structure::=content$_{static}$

Dynamic content represents temporal or asymmetric logical relationships which are irreversible. By irreversible, we mean that the reversed expression of the represented semantics marks a different semantic from the not reversed expression.

$$content_{dynamic}::=<\{REL_{irreversible}\}^*, \{element\}^*>$$

2.2 Typed Resources of DIKW

Towards processing the requirement content, we need to formalize the semantics of the content. We denote target semantic content with resources (RES).

$$RES::=<content_{static}, content_{dynamic}>$$

We category types of resource completely as Typed Data, Typed Information, Typed Knowledge and Typed Wisdom enlightened by the DIKW architecture as is shown in Fig. 1.

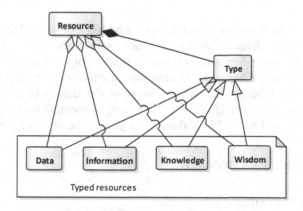

Fig. 1. Basic model of typed resources

$$TYPED_{RES}::=< Typed\ Data,\ Typed\ Information,\ Typed\ Knowledge,\ Typed\ Wisdom >$$

We elaborate the semantic of the elements of Typed Resources in the following sections.

Investigation on the formal semantic of Data, Information, Knowledge and Wisdom in DIKW architecture has long been posed as a big challenge for further investigations on the top of this architecture. Enlightened by the existence vs. identification level modeling perspective [5], empirically we summarized a conceptualization process for DIKW architecture as is shown in Fig. 2 with UML notations of Generalization, aggregation, composition and implementation.

The modeling starts from the observation of the real world which comprises objective observable existence of things. The focus centers the couples of "Entity vs. Relationship" as both objects of observations and elements for expression of observations, and "Identification vs. Notation" of which Identification marks the observed or

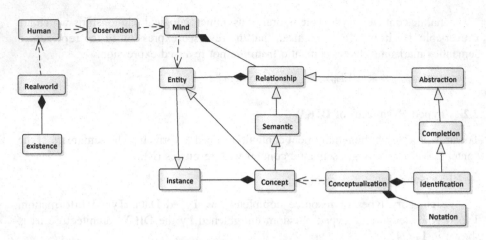

Fig. 2. Model of the conceptualization process

reasoned result of either sameness or difference, and Notation is used to explicitly give an exist symbol for an Identification. Identification on the sameness can be summarized to implement Abstraction. Semantic is based on relationship of entities which confirms to the intent of a human. Concept by its unity can be classified as Entity. Entity inherits instance since entity is judged instances in terms of the identity of its Unity.

We cognitively defined things (THG) as covering elementary targets of observation of a human represented by HUMAN (hmn) at a given time of t. We denote a specific thing as THG (thg).

$$THG(thg)::=OBSERVATION_{HUMAN(hmn)}(t)$$

2.3   Meta Model of DIKW

Figure 3 shows the Meta model of DIKW elements based on extension of Fig. 2. Observations are conceptualized as with representations of identification of ID after a cognitive process of judgement on that whether this specific new thing of THG(thgN) is the same as or different from existing labeled thing of THG(thgE). If the evaluation of the sameness of the THG(thgN) through function of SameAs is positive, the ID of the THG(thgN) will be assigned with the ID of the THG(thgE). Otherwise a new identification will be created with a function of CreateID for THG(thgN).

ID(thgN)::=
(?SameAs(THG(thgE), THG(thgN)), ID(THG(thgE)), CreateID(THG(thgN)))

We define Data in our DIKW architecture as necessarily comprising an existence level prerequisite of an confirmed observation of existence, $Existence_{prerequisite}$ or EX_{pre} and a post-requisite of identification or label of ID_{pst}.

Data::=<EX_{pre}, ID_{pst}>

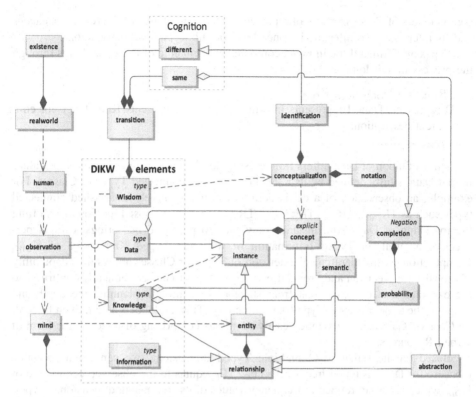

Fig. 3. Meta model of Data, Information, Knowledge and Wisdom

Here an observation means cognitively matched an output of mind thinking process either directly to existing concepts of THG(thg) or indirectly linked existing THG (thgN) as an evidence of the existence of a target of observation.

OBSERVATION(EX(THG(thg)))::=
LinkDR({THG(thg)}) OR LinkIDR({THG(thg)})
EX_{pre}::=EX(OBSERVATION(EX(THG(thg))))
ID_{pst}::=EX(ID(THG(thg)))

Based on this refined semantic of Data, we proposed the concept of Typed Data of D_{DIK} which is the foundation of our proposed Typed Resources (TR) of TR_{DIK} in the DIKW architecture. Our main innovation starts from proposing "Typed Data" as that modeling Data as defined purely by multiple dimensional related "Type (TR)" or "Class" which represents all shared recognizable commons of all subordinate instances of INSs.

TR_x::=ALL(OBSERVATION(THG(thg(x))))

By ALL, it covers unlimited amount of existing or not existing instances. Judgement on whether an INS belongs to a Type will decide the applicability of the operations and rules of the related Type. We denote Typed Knowledge as relying on the completeness of Types in terms of representing the consistency of the related instances and its interactions to infer the instance level or sub Type level associations.

Types are formed through given completeness semantic of the same things through the process of Wisdom.

$TR_{DIK}: = <D_{DIK}, I_{DIK}, K_{DIK}>$
D represents Data, I represents Information and K represents Knowledge for convenient description.
$D_{DIK}::=<TR_x>$

This definition of Data differs from existing modeling of data as instances or values in that Data is fully defined by its related or observed connected Types or Classes. For example, an observation of a cat is defined by its cognitively established connected types such as TR_{color}, TR_{size}, $TR_{sexuality}$, TR_{age}, etc. Our proposed ideology of shifting the modeling of Data from instance or values to purely Types brings a novel perspective as well on Typed Information of I_{DIK} and Typed Knowledge of K_{DIK}. Computationally the hierarchical extension of Types or Classes allows the adaptability of the attained precision and probability of correctness to be economically confirmed to the expected cost or investment from stakeholders, through planning the depth and scope of the to be traversed Type/Class hierarchy. This model of Value Driven tradeoff on Cost vs. Gain can be extended easily to graphs comprising of nodes in the form of Typed Resources.

Based on the semantic of multiple Typed dimensions, we can extend a value measure for D_{DIK} as typed frequency, TF_D. TF_D equals to the observed occurrence of D_{DIK} which is further refined to frequency values of its composing dimensional Types.

$D_{DIK}::=<(Type,TF_D)>$

We can further infer probability of D_{DIK}, represented Pr_D, based on TF_D through enforcing the probabilistic conditions.

The concept of Information is used to represent the Identifications ID of things THG(thg), originating in D_{DIK}, based on the judgement of the Sameness with the confirmation of the Difference.

$I_{DIK}::=<REL_{Difference}(ID_x)>$

The concept of Knowledge is used to represent the application of Completeness semantic which accompanies the semantic of Type as representing the Sameness set of Instances, in the form of Deduction which brings the patterns of Type level to Instance level or Induction which leverages instance level observation with Completeness through Abstraction to patterns of Type level. We count deduction only as a form of mechanism which doesn't require Typed Knowledge in the basic form.

$K_{DIK}::=<REL_{Sameness}(Pattern(Induction, Deduction))>$

The concept of Wisdom, W_{DIK}, is used to represent the modeling and reasoning of the variability and tendency of the change of Typed resources based on patterns or probability crossing cutting Types.

$W_{DIK}::=<REL_{Crosscut(Type)}(Variability(Pattern, Probability))>$

2.4   Connectives of Typed Resources

Based on above formalization, we propose the connectives of Typed Data, Information, Knowledge and Wisdom as is shown in Fig. 4. It further organizes the core concepts of Negation in relation to True vs. False originating in observation on Existence, Completeness in relation to Yes vs. No originating to judgement on Abstraction or Induction, Sameness in relation to quantity of frequency of Typed Data. A refinement of the connectives for Type/Class in terms of Object-Oriented attribute and method is shown in Fig. 5. A further extension of Fig. 5 is shown in Fig. 6 with added explanatory elements.

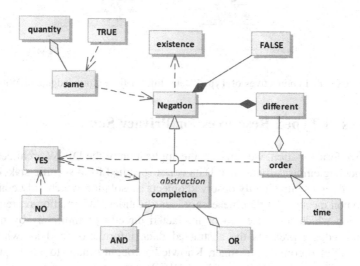

Fig. 4. Connectives of Typed Data, Information, Knowledge and Wisdom

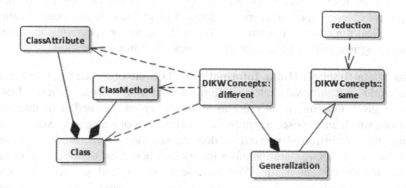

Fig. 5. Refinement of connectives

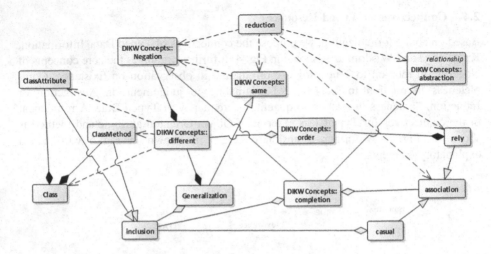

Fig. 6. Extended connectives of Typed Data, Information, Knowledge and Wisdom

3   Graphs of Typed Resources for Privacy Solution

Beside above formalization, we can easy the application of the DIKW architecture with manual modeling empirically as that: Data is not specified for a specific stakeholder or a machine and represents directly observed objects as isolation which only contains the shared common meaning of their necessary identifications. Information represents data or information which are observed or interacted directly or indirectly by human or things. Knowledge represents the abstracted data, information and knowledge in a limited or unlimited complete manner. Knowledge roughly maps to what Kant called Categories [8]. To manipulate the graphs in DIKW architecture, we need to mediate the bidirectional feasible transformations of resources among different types of Data, Information and Knowledge. Schemas [8] are proposed by Kant to cognitively mediate the cognitive objects/experiences mostly through logical reason and concretization in time or logical dimension. We have borrowed this term for specifying the transformation among resources with a focus on the type level implementation.

Schema "Data-Resource (Data, Information)": Data are observed by observers from outside world or from inside categorization on a set of resources, structured or not, which are given the conceptual unity as an entity, or on abstraction of information expressions which are exposed as temporal association among elements. Since resource elements can be abstracted upward or decomposed downward, the expressions of specific DG_{DIK} and IG_{DIK} are therefore intertwined based on the overlapping of the elements and their relationships. We propose to justify and predict the semantic meaning and semantic associations corresponding to resource element expressions based on the reasoning and calculation in a bottom up manner from composing elements of DG_{DIK} and IG_{DIK}.

Schema "Knowledge-Resource (Data, Information, Knowledge)": Knowledge here is either based on the probabilistic experience or based on reason on categories abstracted from directly observed resources or indirectly reasoned resources. A shared characteristic of both forms of knowledge is that they both demand a semantic identification of completeness regardless of whether the actual target resources which are the basis of conceptualization of related categories are limited or unlimited. The schema to enact knowledge on resources is either through temporally decomposing the content of the comprising categories in the knowledge expression as elements shared or can be related to elements in target resources, or through logical or probability reasoning first and decomposing and relating subsequently.

For construction of "Wisdom" related schemas, we adopt the intuition from Schopenhauer [11] to take wisdom as the balancing between reasoning and will for optimizing human long run goals. We omit the discussion on the schema of wisdom here.

We worked towards build "schemas" [8] for DIKW resources for privacy modeling and provision.

DIKWGraph. We specify the usually used concept of Knowledge Graph in three layers of Data Graph (DG_{DIK}), Information Graph (IG_{DIK}), and Knowledge Graph (KG_{DIK}).

DIKWGraph: = $<(DG_{DIK}), (IG_{DIK}), (KG_{DIK})>$.
DG_{DIK}. DG_{DIK}: = collection {array, list, stack, queue, tree, graph}.

DG_{DIK} is a collection of discrete elements expressed in the form of various data structures including arrays, lists, stacks, trees, graphs, etc. DG_{DIK} records basic structures of entities. DG_{DIK} records spatial and topological relationships with frequencies.

IG_{DIK}. IG_{DIK}: = composition$_{time}$ {D_{DIK}}.

IG_{DIK} comprises of temporal relationships based on D_{DIK} with specific scenarios. IG_{DIK} expresses the interaction and transformation of I_{DIK} between entities in the form of a directed graph. IG_{DIK} can record the interactions between entities including direct interaction and indirect interaction.

KG_{DIK}. KG_{DIK}: = collection$_{consistent}$ {Rules$_{Statistic\ OR\ Logical}$}$_{category}$.

KG_{DIK} consistently accommodates either empirical statistical experiences expressed in terms of categories which represent the underlying elements as a whole or completely. Statistic in {Rules$_{Statistic\ OR\ Logical}$}$_{category}$ includes philosophy of Bayesian statistics. Samples of Bayesian classification algorithm may belong to a certain class based on probability.

Typed privacy resources. We formalize privacy resources in Table 1 and we give explanations in campus monitoring system. We define typed resources as a triad:

PR_{DIK}: = $<PD_{DIK}, PI_{DIK}, PK_{DIK}>$.

Table 1. Definitions of privacy resources

Type	D_{DIK}	I_{DIK}	K_{DIK}
Privacy	$\mathbf{PD_{DIK}}:=\{Pdx_1,Pdx_2...Pdx_n\}$	$\mathbf{PI_{DIK}}:=\{Pix_1,Pix_2...Pix_n\}$	$\mathbf{PK_{DIK}}:=\{Pkx_1,Pkx_2...Pkx_n\}$

Explicit and implicit privacy resources. We further categorize target privacy resources of data and information according to their presence in searching space as explicit and implicit. Figure 7 shows our proposition of the semantic of Explicit as directly related to Existence of Typed Data by way of Entity, and Implicit as although mapping to relationships but not directly related to Existence of Typed Data by way of Entity.

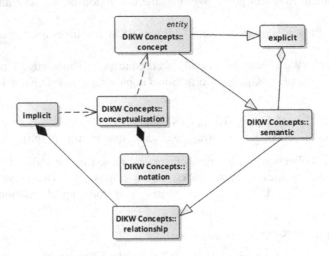

Fig. 7. Semantic of explicit vs. implicit

We proposed to list mark the cost of Type level transition for per unit of source content as is shown in Table 2.

Table 2. Atomic cost of transforming unit resource

	D_{DIK}	I_{DIK}	K_{DIK}
D_{DIK}	$SUnitCost_{D-D}$	$SUnitCost_{D-I}$	$SUnitCost_{I-K}$
I_{DIK}	$SUnitCost_{I-D}$	$SUnitCost_{I-I}$	$SUnitCost_{I-K}$
K_{DIK}	$SUnitCost_{K-D}$	$SUnitCost_{K-I}$	$SUnitCost_{K-K}$

We categorize typed implicit and explicit privacy resources in DIKW Graphs. We conclude an interpretation table shown as Table 3.

Table 3. Preparation of description terms

Term	Interpretation	Term	Interpretation
○	Explicit data resources	☐	Explicit knowledge resources
●	Implicit data resources	■	Implicit knowledge resources
◌	Transformed D_{DIK}	⊡	Transformed K_{DIK}
△	Explicit information resources	→	Connection in resources
▲	Implicit information resources	---ɜ-	Existed resources
△	Transformed I_{DIK}	→	Add new resources

Figure 8 shows the flow chat of creating requirement specification modeling in DIKW Graphs. Users provide requirement specifications. We optimize requirement specifications through analyzing feasibility of target explicit and implicit privacy resources (A), enhancing consistency of explicit and implicit resources (B), eliminating redundancy of explicit and implicit resources (C), and enhancing completeness (D).

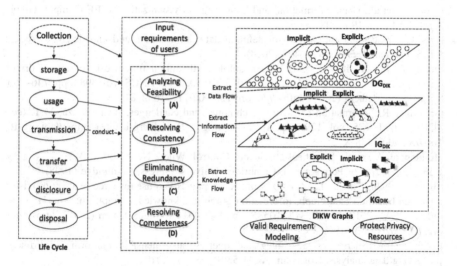

Fig. 8. Flow chat of creating requirement specification modeling in DIKW graphs.

4 Conclusion

In this work, we proposed a formalization of the semantic of the DIKW (Data, Information, Knowledge, Wisdom) architecture. The formalization centers the ideology of modeling Data as multiple dimensional hierarchical Types related to observable existence of the Sameness, Information as identification of Data with explicit Difference, Knowledge as applying Completeness of the Type, and Wisdom as variability prediction of typed Data, Information, Knowledge and Wisdom. Based on this formalization, we modeled the security and privacy content as typed resources of Data, Information, Knowledge and Wisdom. Then base on the difference of the Type transitions among different Typed resources and the difference of the processing cost of converted expressions of target content, we proposed a solution framework which permits Value Driven application of protection functionalities and quality in accordance with the planned investment from stakeholders.

Acknowledgement. We acknowledge Hainan Project No. ZDYF2017128, NSFC under Grant (No. 61363007, No. 61662021, and No. 61502294), Zhejiang Province medical and health science and technology platform project No. 2017KY497. *refers correspondence.

References

1. Appelt, D.E.: FASTUS: a finite-state processor for information extraction from real-world text. In: Proceedings of IJCAI 1993, pp. 1172–1178 (1993)
2. Pearson, P.D., Hansen, J., Gordon, C.J.: The effect of background knowledge on young children's comprehension of explicit and implicit information. J. Literacy Res. **11**(3), 201–209 (1979)
3. Chen, M., et al.: Data, information, and knowledge in visualization. IEEE Comput. Graph. Appl. **29**(1), 12–19 (2008)
4. Zins, C.: Conceptual approaches for defining data, information, and knowledge. J. Assoc. Inf. Sci. Technol. **58**(4), 479–493 (2014)
5. Duan, Y., Fu, X., Hu, Q., Gu, Y.: An ontology definition framework for model driven development. In: Gavrilova, M.L., et al. (eds.) ICCSA 2006. LNCS, vol. 3983, pp. 746–755. Springer, Heidelberg (2006). https://doi.org/10.1007/11751632_81
6. Grishman, R.: Information extraction: techniques and challenges. In: Pazienza, M.T. (ed.) SCIE 1997. LNCS, vol. 1299, pp. 10–27. Springer, Heidelberg (1997). https://doi.org/10.1007/3-540-63438-X_2
7. Hundepool, A., et al.: Statistical Disclosure Control. Wiley, New York (2012)
8. Kant, I.: Critique of Pure Reason. Cambridge University Press, Cambridge (1998)
9. Shao, L., Duan, Y., Cui, L., Zou, Q., Sun, X.: A pay as you use resource security provision approach based on data graph, information graph and knowledge graph. In: Yin, H., et al. (eds.) IDEAL 2017. LNCS, vol. 10585, pp. 444–451. Springer, Cham (2017). https://doi.org/10.1007/978-3-319-68935-7_48
10. Frank, D.: McSherry: privacy integrated queries: an extensible platform for privacy-preserving data analysis. Commun. ACM **53**(9), 89–97 (2010)
11. Schopenhauer, A.: The world as will and representation. Kenyon Rev. **20**(3/4), 44–46 (1998)
12. Soria-Comas, J., Domingo-Ferrer, J.: Big data privacy: challenges to privacy principles and models. Data Sci. Eng. **1**(1), 21–28 (2016)
13. Duan, Y., Shao, L., Hu, G., Zhou, Z., Zou, Q., Lin, Z.: Specifying architecture of knowledge graph with data graph, information graph, knowledge graph and wisdom graph. In: International Conference on Software Engineering Research, pp. 327–332. IEEE (2017)
14. Aamodt, A., et al.: Different roles and mutual dependencies of data, information, and knowledge—an AI perspective on their integration. Data Know. Eng. **16**(3), 191–222 (1995)
15. Tarr, P., Ossher, H., Harrison, W., Sutton Jr., S.M.: N degrees of separation: multi-dimensional separation of concerns. In: International Conference on Software Engineering, vol. 3, pp. 107–119. IEEE (1999)

Correction to: Testbeds and Research Infrastructures for the Development of Networks and Communities

Honghao Gao, Yuyu Yin, Xiaoxian Yang, and Huaikou Miao

Correction to:
H. Gao et al. (Eds.):
Testbeds and Research Infrastructures for the Development
of Networks and Communications, **LNICST 270,**
https://doi.org/10.1007/978-3-030-12971-2

The original version of the book unfortunately contained a mistake in the book title. The title of the book has been corrected.

The updated version of the book can be found at
https://doi.org/10.1007/978-3-030-12971-2

© ICST Institute for Computer Sciences, Social Informatics and Telecommunications Engineering 2019
Published by Springer Nature Switzerland AG 2019. All Rights Reserved
H. Gao et al. (Eds.): TridentCom 2018, LNICST 270, p. C1, 2019.
https://doi.org/10.1007/978-3-030-12971-2_11

Author Index

Printed in the United States
By Bookmasters